To

J. M. Groton.

from

Harry P. Nichols.

C0-AVA-518

THE CHURCH AND ITS AMERICAN OPPORTUNITY

THE MACMILLAN COMPANY
NEW YORK · BOSTON · CHICAGO · DALLAS
ATLANTA · SAN FRANCISCO

MACMILLAN & CO., Limited
LONDON · BOMBAY · CALCUTTA
MELBOURNE

THE MACMILLAN CO. OF CANADA, Ltd.
TORONTO

THE CHURCH
AND ITS AMERICAN
OPPORTUNITY

PAPERS BY VARIOUS WRITERS READ AT
THE CHURCH CONGRESS IN 1919

New York

THE MACMILLAN COMPANY

1919

All rights reserved

Copyright, 1919
By THE MACMILLAN COMPANY
Set up and printed.   Published July, 1919,

262. 4
P944c
1919

151992

CONTENTS

PART IV

ESSENTIALS OF PRAYER BOOK REVISION

PART V

THE NEED OF AN AMERICAN LABOUR PARTY

PART VI

NECESSARY READJUSTMENTS IN THE TRAINING OF THE MINISTRY

INTRODUCTION

THE papers in this volume were read at the thirty-fifth Church Congress in the United States, which was held in Synod Hall in the Close of the New York Cathedral on April 29 and 30, May 1 and 2, 1919. The Bishop of New York opened the Congress with an impressive address, and the Bishop of Erie preached a notable sermon. Within three weeks, the Bishop of New York had entered the new Life: his opening of the Church Congress was, therefore, one of his last official acts. With all others who knew him, we mourn him.

On the first Monday morning of each month during the Spring, Autumn, and Winter, the executive committee of the Congress have met in the study of Grace Church Rectory, New York, to prepare the programme and to elect the writers. Those who have been present (many of them at every meeting) are the Rev. C. Malcolm Douglas, the Rev. George William Douglas, D.D., the Rev. Milo H. Gates, D.D., the Rev. Robert Rogers, Ph.D., the Rev. Theodore Sedgwick, William C. Sturgis, Esq., Ph.D., the Rev. Selden P. Delany, D.D., the Very Rev. Dean Fosbroke, D.D., the Rev. John M. Ericsson, the Rev. William Austin Smith, D.D., the Rev. Floyd W. Tomkins, D.D., the Rev. C. F. J. Wrigley, D.D., the Rev. F. W. Crowder, D.D., the Rev. Charles L. Gomph, the Rev. Harry P. Nichols, D.D., the Rev. Charles E. Hutchison, the Rev. J. Townsend Russell, D.D., the Rev. George R. Van De Water, D.D., the General Secretary (the Rev. Gustav A. Carstensen, D.D.), and the General Chairman. These meetings have been happy occasions when men of differing churchmanship and differing temperament have sought to decide what are the most important problems before the Church, and what men are best qualified to bring out the convictions from the extreme right to the extreme left which are known to exist within the loyalty of the Church. Of course not all who are invited are able to come, and many readjustments are necessary before the programme is complete. For instance we had expected Dean Hodges and the Bishop of Chicago. One was detained by the illness which resulted in his lamented death; the other was called abroad by his duties to the Commission on Faith and Order. It is interesting to note that when the programme was finally announced, every writer appeared to read his paper.

A common conviction that free discussion is a benefit to the Church makes of the executive committee a pleasant and fruitful club. There is, moreover, the sympathetic search for the young man who has shown to his neighbours growing power, and who may find in the Church Congress perhaps his first opportunity for expression to the Church at large. It is encouraging that more of these men of promise are discovered than can at once be invited to a place on the programme, but they are not forgotten. Many of us remember gratefully that the Church Congress brought to us the beginning of a wider influence.

The papers in this volume are printed as they were presented by their writers, with no attempt at editing. What is desired is not a rounded, self-consistent book, but a wholesome array of opinion which may first show what men who care for the Church and religion in America are thinking, and then may be suggestive towards the formation of earnest thought in the minds of those who resemble either Nicodemus or Gallio.

Therefore we send the papers out not as a report but as a book, that in this closing year of a great war there may be in America this record of the reaction of religious men upon the problems which confront the Christian Church.

CHARLES LEWIS SLATTERY,
General Chairman

Grace Church Rectory,
New York,
20 *May*, 1919

PART I

THE EFFECT OF THE WAR ON RELIGION

THE CHURCH AND ITS
AMERICAN OPPORTUNITY

THE EFFECT OF THE WAR ON RELIGION

By WILLIAM AUSTIN SMITH

MANIFESTLY it is too early to measure the permanent effects of the war. We in this generation stand on disadvantaged ground, so sentimentally sketched by Matthew Arnold, too late for the old, too early for the new. However, I think we are persuaded that most of the sermons which we preached in the first year of the war were patriotically commendable, but that as interpretations of religion they left much to be desired. We recall what Dr. Jacks wrote in 1914: "The nations at war are finding their souls." That in general was the thesis of our war sermons. It is an immoral thesis, and the numerous homiletical changes which we rang upon that theme did grave damage to the cause of religion. For it proceeded upon a dangerous assumption—that the ecstacy and romanticism accompanying war are emotionally identical with the Christian experience of the Cross. There is an infallible test of how far our emotions in periods of emotional tension are Christian—how much love is there in our hearts, love of friends and enemies, countrymen and aliens, such love as Christ felt upon the Cross? We are reminded by an English journal that the greatest saying of the war is that of Edith Cavell: "Patriotism is not enough."

To my mind it was a serious blunder that the Church appeared to confuse patriotism with religion throughout the war. Only a few voices in the churches made clear the teaching of Christianity—that war is a loathsome, diabolical disease; that it kills romance and compassion, and finally slays the very soul of justice. The Church need not have attuned its message to an invertebrate pacifism to have uttered that pronouncement. It needed merely to proclaim its christian definitions.

I think it heartless, unchristian, and indecent for clergy and philosophers to glow over the spiritual benefits of a war that laid seven million boys in their graves, starved and maimed from twenty to thirty million human beings, and bathed the world in hate and darkness. I cannot share the easy enthusiasm of these gentlemen. I see in this war a tragedy pathetic beyond words or tears. The Church would do well to leave war in the unpretentious category where General Sherman placed it.

Therefore, by way of preface and definition, I utter my dissent from the popular conviction that war stimulates religion. If I believed that, I should not support a League of Nations to prevent the recurrence of this process of redemption, and to deprive peoples of so ready a means of grace.

We are in a poor mood to meet the returning soldier unless we get this definition clear, for I have found that no body of Christians is so nauseated by the emotional finery with which the Church has decked the carcass of war as the soldier himself. The Christ with a sword in hand going over the top is not the beloved figure that the soldier wants most to meet in churches when he returns. It is the Christ with a cross on His shoulder, healing by love the wounds that sin and folly have made in man's life on earth.

But it is unsafe to assume that because war is a ghastly disgusting business, therefore no good can come from it. Some marvellous by-products have come forth from sin and suffering. Men's wills are free, and the providences of God are fertile with grace. The war has made some serious breaches in religion that will need repairing. I shall not pause to dwell upon these. Neither shall I try to appraise all the benefits claimed for religion by our war workers in France. One bishop I recall, hailed it as a sign of a deepening hold on the realities of religion that our soldiers liked to wear amulets. That kind of testimony has been flooding the home market. I do not think that Protestantism has permanently riveted its affection upon amulets.

We shall take note briefly of three wholesome religious by-products of war. First, it has forced Christianity to define some of its enthusiasms. I think that I was no more muddle-headed in this matter than the average preacher during the war, but I suppose I used the phrase "A new world" in describing war benefits as often as did any of my brother parsons, and with as much confidence that I knew what I meant. But what did we mean? I should like to put that question to the rectors of our great city churches, and to the House of Bishops.

Had we any idea of what *kind* of world we wanted? I ask this, because soon we shall need to pass judgment upon the kind of world we are getting. If the new world is here, most of us would confess that it isn't so awfully nice after all. If the new world hasn't arrived out of chaos, which of the ambassadors and heralds of things new bear the credentials of the Kingdom of God? Most of our vestries will say that the less of a new world we get the better. To them some of the flashes on the horizon are not at all a delightsome thing.

Now, there are groups of thinkers that have a pretty firm idea of what they mean by a new world. I could name several New York weeklies that can tell us precisely what the new world means to them and how to get it. Lenine can tell us. So can Mr. Wells, Bernard Shaw, Bertrand Russell, and Arthur Henderson. The Bishop of Oxford and many another English prelate could, if pressed to do so, give a definite idea of the spiritual quality of that newness. Not that these definitions agree with one another, but my point is that they do not merely state amiable principles; they announce programmes.

It is imperative that religion should know what its enthusiasms mean. We are definitely committed by our war sermons to get something holy out of this welter of blood and ruin. That is why we blessed it, builded our hopes upon it. We said, we will transmute its tears and agony into redemption. Its curses and its blood, its lust, its mangling of the helpless shall be made to sing the glory of God. A new world was the prayer that broke

from a million throats in our churches. Did it mean anything?
We are all of us susceptible to phrases, and yet I think we did
mean something—but what?

I say this in no captious mood. I am asking for information.
One incalculable benefit of the war is that it is going to force
the Church to make some definitions and to take sides in the
great social movement now sweeping the world. Anyone with
any historical perspective knows that the war was not produced
solely by Treitschke, Neitzschke, and Bernhardi. It had its
roots where most modern wars have been made, in the competitive markets of the world. This must be said without
passion, for our whole civilization staggers under the guilt of
this war. But no matter where and by whom the war was made,
when it arrived there was a right and a wrong. The tragedy
linked to nearly all moral problems is that the issue is always
streaked. Its holiness or its sin never comes full circle. But
loyal men must choose. We choose, and while we fought we
made promises to our children, spacious, ecstatic, wondrous.
One of those promises was that a new order should emerge on
earth, one more beautiful, kindlier, cleaner, more Christ-like.
Was this the stuff dreams are made of? Or was it a prayer out
of the deep places of our Christian conscience?

I count it, then, a definite spiritual asset of the war that
it has forced the professors of Christianity to see the new issue
and to take sides. What shall be the way of life for men here
on earth? What shall be the fellowship of their work and play,
their suffering and their strivings? There are crucial times when
Christianity is challenged to do more than to announce principles; it must find solutions. We stand today, as we did when
slavery was an issue, in one of the open spaces in history, wind-
swept by the spirit of God, when Christianity must apply its
creed to the wrongs that waste and cramp the lives of men.

Poets, dreamers, prophets of the world are seeing that the
most tragic heresy of the ages is to teach the Incarnation while
in practice we deny the brotherhood of man. The new ortho-
doxy will define heresy in the spirit of the Master's recorded
judgments on the question: Who is my brother? To me, the

most impressive sermon on the Incarnation ever preached is Edwin Markham's "The Man With a Hoe."

The war, then, has forced religion to define some of its enthusiasms; but it has also revealed to organized religion that some of its enthusiasms are not edifying. A few months ago an article appeared in the *New Republic* entitled "Will Christianity Tolerate the Churches?" The only significant thing about the article was that the title contained a rather clever definition and a suggestion. The definition is that Christianity and the Church are not co-terminous, and the suggestion is that perhaps Christianity may be compelled to take over the churches.

Never since the Christ lived among us in the flesh have the majority of men been so firmly persuaded as they are today that there is no other name under heaven by which the race can be saved than the name of Jesus Christ. For the first time in history the plain man in the street knows what the name of Jesus means for the happiness of mankind. Peoples are singing the Magnificat today as a twentieth-century battle-hymn. They have seen the outlines of the Saviour's face against a background of shrieking hate and cruelty—the mighty of earth trampling on the weak. They have seen the selfish stewardship of brain, of power, and of heritage. And suddenly they have known how different Jesus could have made it all. They know now that it is His way or ruin.

Last Christmas the best Christmas sermons that were preached in America were, I believe, editorials in the secular weekly and daily papers. The birthday of our Lord fell upon the world's confusion like a judgment, a consolation, and a promise. Now, when Christianity gets to be preached in the newspaper offices and the streets of our cities, compulsion is upon us to make it quite clear that the real test of our churchmanship, of our theology, and of our services is, Do they give us the mind of Christ? I know fully with what cheap intent one may make such an assertion as that. I think that I discern the difficult entanglements of historical reference, not to be despised, upon which one enters, when like an eagle one presumes to wing his way straight toward the central orb of truth. I am not pursuing essences of religion. But concerning 60 per cent. of the things which the Churches are discussing, is it not true that the plain man in the street can not for the life of him see what they have to do with Jesus Christ? And that same plain man, were the Master Himself to walk our streets, would understand what He meant. When Jesus of the Gospels speaks, men uncover. They do not follow Him, for His sayings are hard, but they know that they are hearing the voice of God. When the Churches begin to elaborate their system, the plain man is confused.

Now it is quite possible not to have any error in one's system of truth, yet to fail utterly to be a vehicle of truth because of a scattering of emphasis. This is how the Church again and again has proved a blundering custodian of the faith once delivered to the saints. We are carrying too much luggage. What we call our deposit of truth has grown too bulky. It saps our energy to guard and display it. The original jewels are all there, but their lustre is obscured by the setting. The world can be saved by about one-fifth of the bulk of religious truth which we apply to its problems. The war, if I mistake not, has shown us that we have left undone the big things in our anxiety over little things. We should not have had a war at all if we had worried as much about covetousness and worldliness as we have worried over certain things which I shall not name. This is precisely what our Lord found true of religion in His day. The question is not whether all the things we teach are true. The point is that it does not matter much whether some of them are true or not. What matters is that the great fact of human brotherhood and love of God, which men on the street are beginning to discern as the paramount Christian issue, shall find its proper emphasis in organized religion.

Christianity ought always to be in the hands of romanticists. The tragic waste of organized religion from the beginning has been that it has so often been administered "by souls prematurely gray," incapable of risk and greatness. Will the institutions which Christianity has fashioned be permitted to impede the spirit, or will the spirit be permitted to go joyfully, fearlessly, carelessly forward to claim the world for Christ? If the heart be warm with the love of Christ we can make a hundred missteps but they will not lead us away from Him. But we may cherish with historical precision the faith once delivered and yet set ourselves squarely athwart His path. The Churches produce pharisaism more naturally than they produce heresy. There would never have been a heretic if there had never been any pharisees, for the love which is in Christ Jesus throws far a circle which, if we let it, will include and win the erring. Never since Christianity started its course has there been the slightest danger from heresy. The tragic danger has been that we have let the pharisee speak for Christ.

I have small hope of Christian unity without a revolution in the Churches. No plan with the face of Christ in it can live under the hostile glances and inhibitions of those who guard the faith. By the time an idea is pronounced safe, it has died of malnutrition. Have we faced the implications of the fact that Jesus did not get on with religious people?

The war, by contrast, has taught us what a superbly beautiful, adventuresome quest the spirit of God is trying to make of man's life on earth. The cause of Christ's impatience, as it seems to me, with the churchmen of His day was that they thought they were dealing with religion when what they were most concerned about had nothing to do with religion at all. They all wanted to keep something that they had; Christ wanted them to get something that they did not have. Ninety-nine per cent. of their interest in religion was consumed in defending positions. What enthusiasm was there left for religion itself, the wistful following of the spirit of God, the willingness to let Him take these lives of ours, all that they love and own, and lead them whether He will.

And finally, the spirit of freedom which the war has loosed in the world war is bound to touch religion. Mr. Wilson with his gift of phrasing, and his sensitiveness to world moods, made clear as the war progressed that it was a war of liberation. The winds of freedom have been blowing through the streets of the world. But the whole world cannot be intent upon acquiring freedom without having that passion for liberty impinge upon religion. The war has taught us that the Church will not be free until it becomes democratic, and by democratic I mean that the laymen shall have a voice not only in its material governance but in its worship, its faith and polity. And by laymen I do not mean ecclesiastical laymen. Nor do I mean merely the men whom we are accustomed to send to General Convention. There are other precincts to be heard from.

The real problem of church unity is not at all, to my thinking, where our committees on unity are focussing their eyes. The problem is how to get back to the churches the unchurched majority of Christians. These people represent the biggest Church in Christendom. Church unity experts seem to take no account of these people except to mourn over them. Do we seek to know what they miss in us, what they are thinking about, or what they have rebelled against? May they not have some essentials of faith worth incorporating into our new unity? Tying together a group of deserted Churches will not make the appeal of those Churches more winning to the men who rejected them.

What does the unchurched man want of religion? He wants religion to explain what it means. We parsons have got off easy heretofore. The Church has got off easy. We never were checked up on our work. Nobody knew whether the men and the women we graduated could pass their examinations. The war camp let the cat out of the bag. Men who had been confirmed were found not to have a ghost of an idea of what it was all about, what the creeds, the sacraments, and the services mean. They had heard sermons and services, but they had not learned from us what the things they were supposed to believe have to do with religion.

The Church of England has made the discovery, hastened by the war, that only a teaching religion is real. By teaching truth, we test it. If it can't be taught, it isn't true. Religion can mouth phrases for ten centuries, but the moment it is compelled to explain their meaning, the measure of their serviceableness is revealed. If the Church from now on should be compelled to teach its truth, it would drop some of its phrasing and change its emphasis. For example, imagine a Christian Church century after century reading on the first Sunday of every new year an epistle in which the word circumcision is repeated twelve times in fifteen lines! Only by a process of liturgical hypnotism can one read the passage with solemnity. One should not undervalue hypnosis as an asset in liturgical worship, but there are limits prescribed by the comic sense.

The democratizing of religion will, perhaps, mean what the democratizing of government has meant, the putting of its offices at the service of plain men. Our sacramental system, our creeds, our liturgy must be made plain to the ordinary man. Democracy asks blunt questions. The time will come when laymen will decide what shall be the entrance conditions to the Church of Christ and who shall have the right to approach the Table of our Lord. We shall be forced to justify the things which we have proclaimed but not taught, the barriers we have erected, but not explained. We have got to tell plain men what we mean, why we exist, and what we have to offer. The war has revealed our confusion of tongues. In the new era, the Church, no more than Governments, can stand upon inherited privilege. It must serve the plain man or the plain man will make a democratic Church. For this benefit the war has made one glad to be alive.

THE EFFECT OF THE WAR ON RELIGION

By JOHN NEHER LEWIS

IN considering this subject of the effect of the war upon religion, let us consider religion as it expresses itself in the institution which from earliest days and at the present time is called the Church.

Has the Church a function to perform in the construction of a new world? In order to answer this question, it is necessary to define the Church. We must go back to those early days when men and women were called by Christ and banded together in His service. With the flight of time and the development of Democracy, differences in men's method of thought and conception of life and worship, manifested themselves and we have many churches, separated by more or less unimportant differences. The essential idea of the Church lies in the call of Christ, and the acceptance of that call on the part of men and women. A church is either alive or dead, depending upon whether or not it is doing the will of Christ. Church life does not depend solely upon ancestry, or declaration of belief, or form of worship, but upon *Service*. Christ likens the Church to His Body. In fact, He says it *is* His Body. It must, therefore, function with Christ; think His thoughts; *do* His work; set its face steadfastly against those things which He opposes, and cast them out utterly. Christ's Church must be absolutely honest, with itself and with the world. It cannot have a name that it is alive and be dead. That is what happened to the church in Laodicea. It cannot profess to be one thing and be another. If it is this dishonest thing, then no matter how honourable its history; no matter how gorgeous the house in which it lives; no matter how prominent the men and women who belong to it are, it is a dead thing, and like all dead things, ought to be buried.

If the Church is the Living Body of Christ in the world, called to do His will, has it a function, then, to perform in this New Age, and if so what is that function? This is a tremendous subject to approach and attempt to discuss in the limits of one paper. Let me say, in beginning such discussion, that I know the Church *has* a function, and I have very definite ideas as to the nature of its mission. That we are living in a New Age has been said so often that it almost sounds platitudinous to repeat it. What do we mean when we say that? We mean that we are living in a time of revolution or reformation. This is indeed the greatest period of reformation in all the history of the world, save one. That one came 2,000 years ago with the coming of Jesus into the world, and the establishment by Him of a new social order. Jesus is the world's one and only Saviour. He saved His own age from destruction and made it possible for all succeeding ages to save themselves through Him. He was the world's greatest Revolutionist. He said that a man could find his life by losing it. He not only told men how to live and die and live again everlastingly, but He *showed* men how to do just that. Then the Great Light burst upon the world and illumined its dark places. Jesus then called men and women to enter into that New Life with Him: to participate in it, to be a part of it with Him; and in those early days they did just that. The early church was established by living Christians who truly followed Christ; who followed Him until it became a generally accepted statement that "the blood of the martyrs is the seed of the Church."

Age succeeded age, and at times the Image of Christ in the world became somewhat obscured. There was always, however, the Living Body of Christ here in the world in the form of men and women who lived the Christ Life. They kept the springs of life pure and sweet, and from them there flowed streams of living water over a dry and arid waste land which would have perished without them. This living witness to Christ which has saved the world from destruction I like to think of as the Church.

These men and women through succeeding ages have expressed themselves differently. Some of them were teachers, some prophets, some evangelists, some ignorant and unlearned men who simply caught the vision of service and obeyed the call of Christ.

Some ages were marked by the rise of formularies and creeds and ecclesiastical machinery, which, however, were only outward expressions of the lives of men and women who kept the world good and pure. Some of the old formularies are relics of a dead past, but we revere them today because they were put forth by saints of God, followers of Jesus, who by their lives helped people to a larger and truer conception of life.

And then came this great 20th century. We may now speak unhesitatingly of the early days of the 20th century as almost the darkest days in history, for, praise God, those days are happily past. The world had waxed fat and become wanton. The vision of Christ had been obscured. That was the condition in the first decade of the 20th century. We speak of this New Age! Let us see that it is but the ushering in again of the old age, the time of Christ. We clothe those old ideas in new phrases: that is all. Safety of Democracy! League of Nations! World Comity! What are these? New ideas? No. They are the old Christian principles which Jesus enunciated long ago and in the defence of which He died. They are the Brotherhood of Man and the Fatherhood of God. Men say we must have a new Social Order, really meaning that we must go back to the old Social Order, as outlined and demonstrated by Christ Himself. The War, that great, dark spectre which has walked abroad during the past four years, and which has brought so much pain and sorrow to hundreds of thousands of homes in the world, becomes a glorious thing when we think of it as the Great Liberator of Men's Souls, and the agency which has brought men and women back to the teachings of Jesus. When I think of that lonely grave in the corner of the woods in France, with the rude cross over it tied with a shoe-string, and those simple words, "He died for democracy," written there by the loving hands of his fellow-American soldiers, I cannot help feeling that that rude cross over the grave of the Kansas boy must tell the world that he had entered into the fulness of the life of Jesus Christ. He had died for that democracy which Jesus established and which the Christian Church has pledged itself to maintain. But, we now know, one of the saddest things about it all is the fact that so many of those blessed boys over there and the boys and girls, and men and women over here, have lost sight of the true force of religion. Churches have become unreal to them. They think of churches as places in which man-made theories about God and Christ and religion are taught. They have come to think, so many of them, that churches are things apart, something in which they may not or cannot have any part. In this they are wrong. I have seen thousands of young men, who were unconscious members of the Christian Church during the past year. They had not entered into its human organization, but they were in very truth a vital part of its spiritual fabric. They have joined the Church of the Eternal God and become members of Christ through the Baptism of Fire and the Communion of Suffering for the good of others, and in the following of a high and holy ideal which has led them through Gethsemane and Calvary to the Resurrection and the Ascension. They may not have said their creed; they lived it; and I, for one, am sure that they have entered into the joy of their Lord. They *are* members of the Church Triumphant, whether or not they formally joined the Church Militant here on earth. Can we not with profit ask ourselves the question whether or not we may have set forth an utterly wrong idea of what a church is and what church membership means and what religion really is.

Jesus warned us long ago of the danger of giving a stone, when hungry men cried out for bread. It is an ever-present danger, and one which the rejuvenated churches of the 20th century must sturggle against with every last ounce of strength they possess. That tragedy has often happened in the past: the Church has handed out stones in place of bread, and some of the very flower of humanity have turned away disappointed. Now, in this wonderful era of reformation, people are coming

back and again are asking for bread. They have come to see the
necessity for religion. "The religious motive is stronger and
deeper than any other with the masses of men, especially in
times of stress and misfortune. Religion counts today as never
before." Men are literally hungry for it, though that hunger is
sometimes unrecognized by the person himself, and generally
unacknowledged. But the religion they want must be real and
strong and soul-satisfying. They must have it. It is their
inalienable right, and the Church must give it to them. If
not, they will look elsewhere for it, find it if they can, or found
a religion of their own.

The first great essential of the religion for which they are
searching is reality. There has been born into the world in
pain and sorrow a deep scorn for everything which is unreal.
The religion of our age, if it endure and if it is to satisfy the men
of this age, must be absolutely honest. The Church has this
religion which will satisfy men's soul-hunger. It was given to it
long ago by Jesus when he established the Church. The old
Jewish Dispensation ministered to the needs of its age. Moses
was an incomparable leader, but the Jewish Church had become undemocratic, and therefore failed to satisfy men's souls.
It was not universal. Jesus brought to that old Dispensation
new Light and new Truth. He quickened it, reformed it. He
came not to destroy, but to fulfill. The Spirit of Jesus must be
brought into this 20th century Church, still Christian, but in a
certain sense undemocratic. There is no one word more prominent in present day vocabulary than the word "democracy."
It is in the very air. The soldiers coming back every week by
the thousand, have been engaged in a war for democracy. They
all agree that they have been fighting for that. In coming back
here the first thing they are going to look for is democracy.
Are they going to find it? They will look for it in the Church.
Is it here? In theory, yes; in practice, alas! sometimes, No.
But we must see to it that Christian democracy is in the Church.
They will look for it in the State. Shall they find it there? Hundreds of thousands of the best young men in the land have come
to think of this country as their country. They sing of is as

"My Country, Sweet Land of Liberty." They have laid their lives on the Altar of their country; thousands of their fellow-soldiers have had their sacrifices accepted. These young men have cheerfully paid the price, knowing that it *is* their country, and they think of it as an orderly democracy in which they are to have a voice. I have no fear as to their loyal attitude towards their country. They will have neither part nor lot in Bolshevism or anarchy. I say, then, that the first function of the Christian Church in this so-called New Age is to show men and women everywhere the democracy which the Age demands. Caste, either social or religious or ecclesiastical, has absolutely no place in religion. Men will not tolerate it. There is no more blighting, killing thing which can rest upon a church today than that self-sufficient contentment with itself as an institution, which leads it to patronize the ones who come to it for help. The Church must lead the people, teach them, feed them, help them. It can do just this. It has a limitless, divine Source of Inspiration in the life, words, and works of Jesus. The Church must hold up a torch in the world if it is to be real. There is a vast deal of darkness in the world. Jesus Christ *is* the Light. The time is past when people will listen to statements concerning foolish, insipid drivelings of weak, human beings about the infallibility of Mother Church. If the Church would mother the world, it must function as a Mother; it must suffer, and support, and succour the world. The only infallibility of any church lies in the infallibility of its Divine Head, Jesus Christ. Only in so far as the Church holds Jesus up before the world can it truly lead the world.

And now I want to introduce an idea about the Church which is very old. It has been often spoken of before, but it needs to be repeated. It is this: the Church is made up of people. The Church is just we people who are here today. It is not a building; it is not a close corporation in which a few chosen souls may gather for sweet communion, fellowship divine, while the great crowd of men and women who cannot or do not think precisely as those of us who have always been in the Church think and feel, remain apart and go on their way indifferent to its appeal. We, all of us, form the Church. We, who have heard and accepted the call of Christ to a higher life are vital parts of the Christian Church. It is not a thing apart from us. It is ourselves. If all men everywhere could only see this truth and accept it! Men say they have not been confirmed, or even baptized: neither had Matthew that day when he sat at the customs office, or Zaccheus when he sat in a tree to see the procession go by with Jesus; but they heard the call of Jesus to a higher life and answered it, and from that very minute they were members of the Church of those called: for, remember, that is what the Church means, The Called of God.

Whoever we are, whatever we are, if we hear a call to these principles of life as Jesus set them forth, and resolve to follow them as best we can, we then become churchmen or church-women. We may or may not be good and zealous and energetic, but, nevertheless, we are the Church. The Church is comprised of people,—not things, or dogmas, or ritual; it is you and you and you and you. If we are weak, then we are making our church weak. If we are selfish; if we fail to do our part in church life and work; if we hold back our support, financial, physical or moral, then is our church weak in proportion, and it is our fault. The Church has kept the world a decent place in which to live. It has not been all it ought to have been, nor is it now; but that is because we are not all we ought to have been or are now. Its faults are ours; its life is ours, because we are the Church. Personally I believe with all my soul in the regularly constituted order which churches have held sacred through all the ages: Baptism, Holy Communion. These we call Sacraments, because Jesus instituted them. Confirmation, an ancient and early Apostolic rite or ceremony, has been a constant custom in the Church for ages past. I cannot see why all men and women do not accept them; but a man cannot read himself out of a church because he has not embraced these and adopted them. Jesus said, Come unto me, all ye that labor and are heavy laden, and I will give you rest. Men came, and were at once a Church. I know that this is not the view of some people concerning the nature of the Church, but I believe it is the fundamental idea of that New Democracy of which men are speaking much today, and for which our soldiers have given their lives and the vision of which they are seeing clearly.

I cannot outline any programme of church activity for the period of reconstruction which lies just before us. I simply say reverently and humbly that the Church has a great function to perform in this wonderful new era which has dawned upon our world, and I believe with all my soul in the absolute necessity for coöperative effort on the part of all Christian people in making the Church a vital force in the New Democracy.

THE EFFECT OF THE WAR ON RELIGION

By John Farwell Moors

ONE who comes from the rock-bound coast of New England and has served for years as clerk of the old First Church in Boston, having in his keeping the original record-book, with its crumbling leather cover and its quaint entries, has abundant reason to respect religious tolerance. For the capital city of Massachusetts has always been a hot-bed of sectarian strife. The original settlers came from the east side of England, where Wycliffe and his followers had repudiated the Roman Catholic Church long before the Protestant Reformation. The Puritans were in turn non-conformists to the once heretical Church of England. In time the Unitarians, who in their early enthusiasm, developed the writers of the Elizabethan age in New England— Longfellow, Lowell, Hawthorne, Emerson, Holmes, Channing, Parker,—broke loose violently from the "orthodox"Congregationalists. I can remember living as a boy in the Connecticut valley with an uncle, who was a Unitarian minister, and hearing the word "orthodox" whispered, as if too dreadful to mention aloud. With the steamship companies stimulating immigration, further violence ensued from a new source. A convent was burned. The public schools became the centre of a struggle between the "A. P. A." (American Protective Association) and the ever growing adherents of the Roman Church. Today that Church is the predominant Church in Boston, though the forefathers of the original settlers seceded from it nearly a thousand years ago. The circle is complete.

One, like myself, who has taken part annually for a quarter of a century in public school elections can testify to the strain and suffering and harm which spring from sectarian strife and can welcome with peculiar earnestness the tendency towards greater Church unity which the war seems to have developed. We have seen the clergy of all denominations working and fighting together for the common causes of the great war. We have seen the boys of all denominations comrades in battle. If I may revert again to my own city, the old First Church in Boston, which had participated in the Unitarian schism, united a year ago with a neighbouring Congregational Church, for the laudable purpose of saving coal. And this reunion was renewed in Holy Week this year. Common causes, more ennobling than sectarian strife, should emerge from the war and tend to bring together all serious-minded men and women. When we reflect that tolerance is the reverse of intolerance, we realize what a great virtue tolerance is.

If it be true that most people uphold their own religious beliefs simply because they were born into them (hardly a certain basis for these beliefs being more infallible than those of other people born into other beliefs) it is even more true that, before the war, there was not a nation in the world which did justice to any other nation. There is not a habit of mind more easily formed and there are few more baneful than the habit of assuming that our ways and customs are the standard and that every divergence from them is reprehensible.

Many years ago I was in a railway car on the wharf at Boulogne with an Englishman—a clergyman, if you please— and certain female members of his family. Putting his head out of the window he called, "Parlez vous français," to a French porter in a blue blouse. The porter hurried to him politely with a few words in French signifying a desire to help. The clergyman threw himself back in his seat and laughed. "I only wanted to hear him do it," he remarked. "To think of anyone actually speaking such a language!" Englishmen know French porters in blue blouses better now. And we Americans know Englishmen and Frenchmen better—we had almost grown to think that we knew Italians and Japanese better. Usually we like people when we know them because man, made in the image of his Maker, is good. If this were not so, life would truly not be worth living. And the war, through bringing many nations together in a common cause, has laid the foundation, through knowledge, for further tolerance.

We have still, however, far to go. We Americans have called new-comers to our land "paddies," "sheenies," "dagos," and "niggers" and we have elegantly called our Mexican neighbours "greasers." The whole presumption of such nicknames is derisive and unfriendly, and hard feelings result. Similarly, patricians and plebeians, capitalists and laborers, look askance at each other. Racially and socially the war seems rather to have intensified than to have reduced the intolerance, misunderstanding, and trouble among great groups of people in America.

The solution, we will all agree, must be found in magnanimity. As a general proposition this seems axiomatic. We know too that it has been true in the past. Every man with magnanimity is in time respected, no man without it can be. Abraham Lincoln has won the heart of everybody. Thad Stevens and Ben Wade, responsible for the hateful reconstruction period after the Civil War, are beloved by no one. Similarly we now sympathize with John Bright's struggles for down-trodden working people and for political enfranchisement. But these are admirations for men in another age. What is plain to us now because it is past was not plain to people then when it was present. When we face our own world reconstruction problems, our own factory system, our own clamorers for more democracy, the solution, through magnanimity, is not so manifest. No solution seems obvious and our hearts are more easily hardened than softened. In the present it is so much pleasanter to be on good terms with the respectable and the conventional than to take one's chances with the Lincolns and the Brights before they have been accepted into the select company of heroes! It is also much pleasanter to indulge in the heroism of bands of music and applause and reception committees than to face alone that other kind of heroism, which must be painful, or it would not be heroism.

We tend to disagree as we become specific. We have today an elastic word "Bolshevist," which, in that it is always with us, seems to be a sort of poor relation of "camouflage." The word "Bolshevist," as applied to educated Americans, seems to signify anyone who dares to think a hair's breadth more liberally than his friends. Here then, after the war, we see cropping up the same kind of intolerance as has, since the beginning, embittered people in my native city, and has everywhere caused international jealousies and hatreds, revengeful class distinctions, racial antipathies. Most of us have long been slaves to the fetish of large scale production. Suddenly intense human demands supplant the whir of mill machinery; and individuality, almost crushed in millions working monotonously, struggles violently to assert itself. There is today a strike at Lawrence. Outsiders interesting themselves in that strike are far from being admired as John Bright is admired, but are practically ostracized. Today too a peace conference is sitting, and the whole world has been hushed, awaiting the outcome. Suddenly there is a public clash between the old order and the new, between Italy and America. At such a juncture a banker, like myself, asks himself how far the Church is upholding spiritual truths and pointing the way. Has the Church the vision and the courage which can make true leadership possible? Has the war lifted us all to a higher level or has it perchance, through intolerance, debased the purposes of men and made their relations with one another more unfriendly and sinister?

I was in a well-known Church on the Sunday after the armistice was signed. The preacher, in naval uniform, and popular, had before him a congregation electric with pent-up emotion. He dwelt on the German atrocities, known, alas! by all of us, and, while he admitted in that house of Christian worship that vengeance belonged to the Lord, he made the admission with so wrathful a manner that the implication was strong that it would be desirable, not to say dutiful, to participate vigorously on the Lord's side during the infliction. I noted that every eye was hard, for no heart had been touched. Why did this preacher in our day of rejoicing seek to harden our hearts?

Last week, nearly six months after the armistice was signed, I read three newspaper columns reproducing an address given by the pastor of one of the best known churches in New York. The article is entitled, "Another Crucifixion." This clergyman said: "Now Russia is being crucified by Trotsky and Lenine. Her land has become a land of trampled corn-fields and bloody streets. Oftentimes—almost before they have buried their victims, the murderers have quarelled like cats and dogs over the division of the spoil. Bolshevik leaders, armed with machine guns, enter the city and loot the houses upon one street and live upon the accumulated spoil; the next week they loot another street. Corpses lie frozen or festering in the alleys. From time to time the Bolshevists played a battery of machine guns on some quarter where a handful of citizens were defending their wives and daughters." And so on through the three columns. Why is this picture made so hateful? The clergyman who paints it is not bringing us first-hand evidence—that is not conclusive one way or the other as to the facts—but he seems to paint the picture in such a way that our hearts may indeed be full of hate. He would also make us afraid, for he says: "The spread of Bolshevism is alarming to the last degree. Today it has become a menace to our own country." The logic seems to be that safety lies in hate.

At this point of our analysis of the effect of the war on religion, let us set before ourselves the two fundamental commandments given us in the Gospels: "Thou shalt love the Lord thy God," and "Thou shalt love thy neighbour as thyself." How unquestioned these commandments were formerly! Before the war, when, so far as we knew, we had no enemies, we had no doubt that, if ever any should appear, we should abide by the Christian doctrine, that we should love even them. But in the present critical period with its complications, cross-currents, onimous contentions, deafening noises, monstrous wrongs, horrors, may it be that Dr. Henry Van Dyke at Trinity Church, Boston, at a supreme moment last November, and Dr. Newell Dwight Hillis at Marble Collegiate Church, Manhattan, this month, were justified in their harsh judgment? May it be that the two great commandments of the Saviour do not apply to such human beings as the Germans and the Bolshevists?

There are various avenues of escape from this dilemma. We can take the broad path of following the trend of public opinion, the path of saying what those who listen to us want to have us say, the path that too often in the end leads to the moral destruction of anyone, clerical or lay, who thus publicly addresses his fellow-beings. I imagine that I was invited here to emphasize, what we all know, that the war has deepened our emotions and has developed in us powers, previously unknown, to do difficult and disagreeable tasks. Past martyrdom is so much more respectable and painless than current martyrdom that I should much prefer to read about the martyrs of the Spanish Inquisition than have any considerable number of people read about my own martyrdom. Nevertheless, I hardly like to escape from my dilemma by the path just indicated. In my own city, certain enterprising newspapers have sought a solution in full-page advertisements, signed by nobody, decrying the Bolsheviki as sweepingly as Dr. Hillis. Typical sentences are: "The old Eagle has his eye on 'em and he's going to sweep 'em out. Every loyal American in every walk of life should help the sturdy beak and talons in the unrelenting fight."

Another way of escape is suggested by an author whose skill is second to none in the now popular art of rousing derisive laughter and who is read and admired by thousands of educated Americans, Mr. George Harvey. He writes with the confidence begotten by abundance of eminently respectable commendation of what he calls "the Hun barbarian hordes" as follows: "The French would be blind indeed did they not insist to the last that the Beast, so long a nightmare and an impending threat of ruin and devastation, be disarmed and shackled and rendered impotent, even as the Beast would have shackled France and rendered her forever impotent, had the Beast and not civilization won on the recent battlefields. It was for that purpose that the war was fought. No wonder the French brand as childish any concessions made to check the spirit of Hun vengeance. The Hun must be so shackled that he will be constrained for generations to take his revenge out in lyrics and not in acts— that is the way and the only way to meet Hun revenge problems.

It is not whether a certain course will modify his desire for revenge, it is whether it will or will not make that revenge impossible. If entangling Commandments (*i e.* the 14 points on the basis of which Germany surrendered) are in the way, chuck them overboard. If sentimental idealisms are obstacles sweep them aside. Shackle the Hun! Tie him up with just enough freedom left to work out his billions of money debt. That debt is but a trifle in the sum total of his wrongs to humanity. The rest can never be paid. It is a dishonored obligation recorded for ever in that brand of infamy that is burned deep and indelibly for all time upon the Hun's shameless forehead."

Certain gentlemen in my profession, meanwhile, would apparently settle the problems now facing the world in a practical and old-fashioned manner. They seemed very tenderly inclined to a budding new revolution in Mexico, a revolution under the nominal leadership of Felix Diaz, with much praise for both the former Diaz and the Huerta regimes and a suggestion of sympathy even for the unspeakable Villa. The new revolution was conceived not only while the present Mexican government seemed to be restoring order but at the very moment when our own government was straining every nerve to lead the world towards new and just international relations, based on respect for the rights of others, notably for the rights of weak nations.

A point of view more in line with the Christian commandments has recently been suggested by Count Ilya Tolstoi, now visiting this country. But the reception of his views here gives an index to one effect of war on religion which it seems to me well to consider. This reception becomes the more significant when we recall the great prestige of the older Tolstoi and the respect which we all felt for him in his later years, during his attempt to reintroduce primitive Christianity. A week ago the *Boston Evening Transcript*, read by all educated New England, had an editorial which is called, "Tolstoism and the Conference." It said: "Count Ilya Tolstoi says that he is a Christian and not a politician. Count Ilya's idea of Christianity is that 'the whole claim of Italy and Japan for annexations should be wiped away,' that 'France should forget her desire for the Sarre

Valley and the Rhine frontier.' The Tolstoian Christianity gives the fruits of victory to the conquered and puts the victor in the future power of the beaten robber nation. The principles of primitive Tolstoian Christianity may be admirable in their application to individuals but they are dangerous in international affairs." We see here what effect this war, which America entered that Christian principles might obtain among nations as among individuals, has had on this influential newspaper and through it on thousands of readers. Either it never outgrew or it has reverted to the old doctrine that to the victor belong the spoils, not merely in political but in international affairs of supreme moment. This general point of view pervades the editorial pages of this paper. At Christmas time this last winter I bought a copy at Providence on my way to Boston from New York. In it I read that a certain "offensive" slogan must be taken down from the State House. Knowing the paper well I looked up this offensive slogan and found that it was: "League of Nations: Peace on Earth. Good-will to men." I cite these instances as they are typical of the effect of the war on the religion of a newspaper which has long been a New England institution.

As a banker I take pride in the recent utterance of a Governor of the Bank of England who said: "I decline to admit that there is anything soft or sentimental in the Golden Rule. It is, on the contrary, the embodiment of sound practical common sense. I repel the idea that there is anything weak or unmanly in the Christian law of forgiveness. On the contrary, its wisdom is justified by the common experience of our every day life. I have yet to meet a man who, in retrospect of life, finds satisfaction in an injury avenged or regret for an injury forgiven."

I once heard a man of true religion, Bishop Brent, tell how no less a man of war than General Pershing was unable to put down an uprising of wild tribes in the Philippines. There are some things, for example influenza, which armies cannot overcome. Bishop Brent asked General Pershing's permission to meet the uprising in his own way. The request was granted. Thereupon the good bishop went to his task armed only with a penknife, plus a power mightier than any army, with love in his heart even for these wild neighbours. When I saw him, the impossible had been accomplished. The uprising was at an end. In place of it there was on the credit side of the ledger a good-will account of immeasurable value.

As we proceed with our analysis are we not constrained to conclude that the tremendous experience of the war has proved that the Law and the Prophets are not to be swept aside in the great crises of life, but are then more than ever applicable? The eternal truths of Christianity have not been shaken by the war. But what shall we say of the attitude of Americans towards them?

Have we not all noted a growing tendency on the part of influential men to brow-beat those who disagree with them? Think of all the epithets which were used during the war! And now that the war is over, the man who stands up against the popular view is usually not allowed when quoted to speak—he squeals, squeaks, shrieks, whines, or whimpers. Whenever I see these verbs applied to anyone I know that injustice is being done, for I know that no one with any moral courage ever expresses himself in such tones. The amount of persecuting now in evidence by those who conceive that it is for righteousness' sake has grown enormously as a result of the repressive rules which had to be enforced during the war and the habits thus formed. At a class reunion the other day in my city those present were asked whether they belonged to a certain liberal club. One man rose and said "Yes." Asked what the club stood for, he replied, "Idealism." Only scorn was thereupon expressed for idealism, no other man daring to stand up with the man attacked. The scorn came as a matter of course, for the spirit of persecution is rampant.

If we examine the practical effects of the doctrines preached by Messrs. Harvey and Hillis, do we not find that the former seeks to protect our civilization of mind and heart and soul by hard physical force, that his programme, if carried out, would leave 40,000,000 Frenchmen next to 70,000,000 enraged Germans, and that it would bring outcast Germany and outcast Russia together in a combination of outcasts with infinite possibilities to damage the rest of the world? And will not Dr. Hillis, if he has his way, create the kind of Russia which will make a partnership with outcast Germany almost inevitable? And will there not be a certain poetic justice in this, for hardness begets hardness, and hate begets hate? To me the counsels of these gentlemen seem infinitely expensive, infinitely brutal, and infinitely dangerous.

If, however, we accept the Christian commandments as eternal and more applicable at supreme moments than at other times, is it possible to overcome with good the evil depicted by these gentlemen? We at least know that the misguided Bolshevists are poor and the Germans beaten, with their wicked rulers swept away. To the poor and the fallen we have at other times assumed that our attitude should be like that suggested by the Governor of the Bank of England whom I have quoted. But at this crucial hour is this our attitude? Again, is there perhaps some virtue even in the Germans and the Bolshevists which Messrs. Harvey and Hillis have overlooked? If so—now is surely the time for the followers of Christ to know it and to act accordingly. I feel sure that you agreed with me when I showed how an English clergyman had failed in courtesy to a French workman on the dock at Boulogne, and when I suggested that we had not done justice to new-comers to this country because we had not understood them, and when I pointed out what evil had been wrought through intolerance in the capital city of the Puritans. Will you now agree with me that it is only through holding out a Christian hand toward the good in other people, even the Germans and the Bolshevists, made like ourselves, in God's image, as Bishop Brent held out his hand to the savage Filipinos, that the evil which is now devastating the world can be overcome?

In other words, have we not reached a point in our analysis where it is plain that now is the great opportunity as well as the great peril of the Christian Church? Men are beginning to say, "We see no resemblance between the views expounded inside the Church and those freely expressed outside it." Some men think they see only a tradition within the Church which would not stand for a moment against the weight of opinion without it, if the tradition were carefully examined. On the other hand, the whole world is today eloquent with the evil which springs from flouting Christianity. Furthermore at this time, when the Harveys and Hillises are heard everywhere, some American statesmen have become the champions of fundamental Christianity. On which side is the Church ranged?

A fortnight ago I heard a most intellectual preacher. After the service an admiring member of his congregation said: "Is he not skilful? He has deep convictions. But he knows that the rest of us do not agree with him. So he makes his points guardedly without jarring anyone." Skill certainly lies that way, but leadership and salvation do not.

Intolerance in high places has reached such a pitch that one cannot with impunity seek the light as to either Germany or Bolshevism. It is hardly safe socially even to mention the Germans or the Bolshevists except to execrate them. Even the strike at Lawrence is so taboo that a well-conducted and useful charity in my city is said to have been hurt because its excellent president made a trip to Lawrence to study the strike there. Intolerance has forced the timid into silence and the fanatic into an intensified sense of grievance. But at this juncture when the least liberality or "idealism" is labelled with the same word, "Bolshevism," as the horrors described by Dr. Hillis, a new adherent for so-called "parlor Bolshevism" has appeared in the not impecunious person of Mr. John D. Rockefeller, Jr. He said last week: "As the leaders of industry face this period of reconstruction, what will their attitude be? Will it be that of the stand-patters who ignore the extraordinary changes which have come over the face of the civilized world and have taken place in the minds of men; who, arming themselves to the teeth, attempt stubbornly to resist the inevitable and incite open warfare with the other parties in industry. Those who take such an attitude are wilfully heedless of the fact that its certain outcome will be financial loss, general inconvenience and suffering, the development of bitterness and hatred, and in the end submission to far more drastic and radical conditions. Apply the Golden Rule to industry. Labor and capital are partners. This attitude, this relationship, is the personal relationship in industry; nothing else will take its place, nothing else will bridge the chasm of distrust and hatred."

Has the Church been as far-seeing and courageous in standing sponsor for a new world order, based on Christian principles, as has either American statesmanship or the two financiers whom I have quoted, who have expressed such loyalty to the Golden Rule? In Mr. Rockefeller's remarks there is, it is true, a note of fear and a warning, based on fear, if the browbeating in high places continues. If salvation is to come, we must all surely have impulses nobler than those founded in fear. For fear usually underlies intolerance. If we hate the Germans, the Bolshevists, and now the "idealists," it is primarily because we fear them. All Europe was in a state of fear before the war in due course resulted. Fear now may again wreck the world.

There is no fear in the Sermon on the Mount. There has been no fear in the magnanimous attitude of certain churchmen, notably in England. The Lord of Hosts was surely with America when we entered the great war and fought for justice and humanity, without fear or any selfish object. Is He not with us now at the Peace Conference, still asking nothing for ourselves but striving steadfastly to open the gates to a new and better word?

Magnanimity! What greater national infirmity have we had, from the days of George Washington to the days of our President, called the worst since Buchanan, than our habit of injustice towards those whom we have elected to our most responsible and difficult office. If the actual facts against them have not sufficed, we, as a people, have resorted to imaginary facts, the more scandalous the better. The war has intensified this national infirmity. We disregard the special prayers with which every week we invoke for him the blessing of the Most High, thus giving additional reality to the doubts of those who have noted the discrepancy between the Christianity preached inside the churches and the Christianity all too palpably not practised outside them.

If we accept the proposition that tolerance and magnanimity are essential to success in solving our present world problems, how shall we rate the attacks on the President first on one side and then on another? Whatever our views as to him, we at least know that he is in Europe in conference with the tried diplomats of Europe, that he has a divided country behind him, that in returning to Europe and taking the stand there which he has taken, he has thrown away his prestige, if his critics may be believed, that his task as stated by himself, is in substance the reintroduction of Christian principles into international relations, and that, during part of his present stay in Paris, he has been ill in bed. Let us compare what a Congressman from Massachusetts, now Speaker of the National House of Representatives and the Hon. James M. Beck have recently said of him to practically the same audience. Said the former, "I do not blame the President for wanting to return to the atmosphere of luxury and adulation which awaited him in Paris." Said the latter: "We read in a recent despach from Paris that our somewhat overworked President was unable to attend a meeting of the Council of four, as on that morning he was giving appointments of fifteen minutes to the delegations from America, Europe, the near East, the Far East, who sought the influence of America in their various problems. He talked to a Chinese delegation about Shantung; listened to some citizens of France on the question of the Rhine frontier; then heard the petition of the Chaldean delegation, then heard the complaint of the Slavic Dalmatians; then gave audience to a representative of San Marino, a mighty nation of some 11,000 people; then conferred with the Swiss minister of foreign affairs; then conferred with a Greek patriarch from Constantinople, and then permitted Essed Pasha to present the claims of Albania. This was followed by a petition from Portugal; then came the minister from Serbia to decide the fate of the Balkans, and the final interview was accorded Frank Walsh, with reference to the claims of the Irish Republic!" This sarcastic summary seems at least to dispel the other critic's charge of a return to luxury! There is not a word of magnanimity from either gentleman for "our somewhat overworked President," as described by Mr. Beck. On the contrary, his conclusion is, "Upon what meat doth this our Caesar feed that he is grown so great?"—words with which Cassius incited Brutus through evil passions to murder Caesar.

What then should be our answer to the question contained in the words, "The Effect of the War on Religion?" We all know that Americans everywhere have left the mighty uplift of our great common cause. According to our lights, we have been ready for any sacrifice. We have not faltered when we could see the way. In those respects we have indeed been exalted. But humbly, heartily, and gratefully granting all this, what are we to say of present fear among those who go to the churches, of the present blindness, the present intolerance, and, may I say it, the brutality in us which has survived the war against brutality in others? Underlying all these baser qualities is the old habit of seeing the motes in the eyes of others. We describe the Germans, the Bolshevists, even the labouring classes here, in the darkest terms, not like people trying to make an accurate diagnosis. Instead of having faith, hope, and charity at this time when they are most needed, instead of claiming our birthright as men, to be a little lower than the angels and by our magnanimity to be crowned with glory and honour, shall we insist on the wretched mess of potage whose chief ingredient is hate? If we make this choice, I submit that in the world-wide conflict now raging between good and evil, we are ranging ourselves on the side of nothing less awful than re-established paganism.

May we not give heed at such a time to the noblest treasures in our English language? Said Hamlet to Polonius: "Good my lord, will you see the players well bestow'd. Do you hear, let them be well us'd?" Polonius replied, "My lord, I will use them according to their desert." Listen then to Hamlet: "God's bodykins, man, better; use every man after his desert, and who should 'scape whipping? Use them after your own honour and dignity; the less they deserve the more merit is in your bounty. Take them in."

Who would have thought before the war that our hearts could be so hardened against anyone that they would not respond with joy to such generosity! Consider also the famous words of Portia, beginning: "The quality of mercy is not strained," especially these lines:

> "But mercy is above this sceptred sway,
> It is enthroned in the hearts of kings,
> It is an attribute of God Himself;
> And earthly power doth then show likest God's
> When mercy seasons justice. Therefore Jew,
> Though justice be thy plea—consider this—
> That in the course of justice, none of us
> Should see salvation; we do pray for mercy.

And that same prayer doth teach us all to render the deeds of mercy."

Have such words as these been in our hearts of late, even though before us lies a world in agony? Yet is not this the time when they most apply?

Two generations ago there was bitterness here as great as now. It was directed against the South, now happily reunited with the North, which then had refused to abolish slavery and had tried to disrupt the Union and had killed hundreds of thousands of our young men. As the Civil War drew near its triumphant end, an inspired American president sought to bind up the nation's wounds "with malice toward none, with charity for all." He did not insist that malice must prevail and charity be postponed until the South had repented. If he had, would the memory of Abraham Lincoln have become our most cherished possession?

Let us try a last test. Should we know Jesus of Nazareth who was crucified because He would not renounce the everlasting truth, and would He know us if we should meet Him alone now in the streets of this vast Babylon? Might He look sadly for His disciples as before, among the poor and the fallen, conceivably even among those whom we despise? What could we tell Him if He should ask us whether or not we have unfalteringly tried to love our enemies and to overcome evil only with good?

I am sure that many here could stand this test. I am sure that they have not only preached but practised tolerance and magnanimity under the most trying circumstances. Please don't misunderstand me. I am not here and now upholding the fallen Germans or the long down-trodden Bolshevists or the masses of poor human beings in our great factories or the President of the United States in his hard mission. But I am urging that elementary Christianity should be our guide in our treatment of all men and women now and for ever. Too many prominent men seem to have lost this guide. I have mentioned certain names only to give reality to the voices which now fill the air. The war has indeed brought us nearer to realities. And the voices of men who have lost their way, but do not know it, must be met by the Church with its appeal to the things which are eternal. Now, when the need is greatest, we must not faint or be weary or utterly fail. For the everlasting truth has been illuminated, not dimmed, by the world tragedy of the last five years.

PART II

SHALL WE RETAIN THE OLD TESTAMENT
IN THE LECTIONARY AND THE SUN-
DAY SCHOOL?

SHALL WE RETAIN THE OLD TESTAMENT IN THE LECTIONARY AND THE SUNDAY SCHOOL?

By Hughell E. W. Fosbroke

TO put a question in its most challenging form is always worth while if it takes us back to first principles. As long as there is only a vague assumption that the Old Testament ought to have its place in Christian worship and education, an assumption often deriving largely from the inertia of traditional views, any intelligent discussion of method is impossible. Obviously what one wants to do must play an important part in determining the way in which it is to be done. Our reasons for retaining the Old Testament, if we can find any, may not at once solve the problem of method, but they may indicate the direction in which the solution is to be sought.

Let us address ourselves to the question of the Lectionary first, for that use of the Bible which marks it as the Church's book should be of large significance for the work of the Sunday-school. In the interest of a really radical treatment of the subject I venture to suggest that we ought to take one further interrogatory step and ask, Why do we have Scripture lessons at all in our services? Is the hearing of God's most holy Word an integral part of worship, or is it something additional representing the purely didactic motive, the skilful insertion of a modicum of instruction in the intervals of prayer and praise? That, it may frankly be admitted, seems to be the principle informing the lectionaries with which we are familiar and is, I believe, an underlying reason for the wide-spread dissatisfaction with them. Judged by the pedagogical standards of today, much of the Bible falls short of that prosaic clarity which the work of instruction seems to demand and our sermons sometimes attain. If edification in the sense that the hearer is to carry away some part of what he has heard as of immediate practical importance is the primary purpose of the reading of the Scriptures, it is not unreasonable to ask that simple and direct applicability, unhampered by the difficulties associated with an alien background, be the first desideratum. The Bible can no more be used as a handy manual of moral maxims than it can be treated as a thesaurus of proof texts. This is as true of the New Testament as it is of the Old. Edification does follow on the liturgical reading of the Scriptures as indeed it can hardly fail to result from prayer and praise and thanksgiving. We praise God and our own life is marvellously enhanced by so doing but if this enhancement is made the very purpose of our praise we are but indulging in a form of self-aggrandizement. We need services, no doubt we ought to have more of them, in which the primary aim is instruction and in these too the Bible, including the Old Testament, will, I believe, play its part. In the lectionary, however, we are concerned with that public worship in which men are brought immediately into the presence of God. And in this the Bible has its place, not first of all because it is edifying, though that is abundantly true, but because it is the Word of God. We are keenly aware for example of the difficulty that attaches to our present use of the Commandments. The sanctions awaken questioning, the prohibitory form is insufficient for the purposes of self-examination such as their use indicates. Read, however, as a lesson, they come as a significant moment in God's revelation of Himself through the moral law, a moment which has present value as we are reminded that the recognition of the "Thou shalt not" is the condition of our understanding the deeper truths of love.

Lest I be thought to be trying to close the discussion by an obscurantist appeal to dogma, let me ask you to consider the significance of what is supposed to be the listening attitude of the congregation while the lessons are being read. Elsewhere in the service, in prayer and praise and thanksgiving whether they speak themselves or one speaks for them, the movement is from themselves Godward. They are drawing near to Him, contritely or joyously, conscious of their need, or, forgetful of self, in some splendid hymn of praise affirming His infinite greatness. Thus far it is all part of "the warm romance of man's pilgrimage to God." We know, of course, that in all the seeking something more than man is revealed. In a very real sense the quest is the answer, but the subjective element predominates. During the reading of the lessons, however, the movement is reversed. Instead of active participation in words and phrases, which in some measure voice their own aspiration they are listening to that revelation of Himself which God has given in the terms of human life. They are reminded that worship is no soaring into the unimaginable void where the mind is entirely free to create because set free from fact, and the heart may identify God with the onrush of its own sanguine impulses. Worship is the keeping of a tryst. The tabernacle of the congregation is the tent of meeting, and God comes, not as we would fondly imagine Him to be, but as One Who, in ways unexpected and sometimes where we should least have looked for it, has made Himself known. Have we not sometimes felt that services of intercession consisting only of litanies and prayers and hymns have missed, I will not say the note of reality, but that sense of actual contact with concrete fact which gives what is more than the assurance of answer to petitions, the conviction that One with will and purpose of His own has taken account of our poor human longings and will do with them what seemeth Him best.

It is the power of the Bible to bring home to us the reality of God that can alone justify its continued use in our services. This is its distinctive ethos, the quality by which it moulds us, and for the wholeness of God's revelation of Himself we need the whole of the Bible, the Old Testament as well as the New. It is true that the Christ is the sufficient revelation of the Father, but it is the Christ in the fulness of His life that thus reveals God, the Christ who in the stress of temptation and in His deepest agony upon the Cross finds the language of the Old Testament come instinctively to His lips, the Christ who in one of His parables makes Abraham say, If they hear not Moses and the prophets neither will they be persuaded though one rose from the dead. It is not simply a question of understanding the background of New Testament times, of making intelligible some of our Lord's allusions, it is a question of the very mind of Christ Himself, our power to see life in some degree as He saw it, in the light of that great revelation of God of which He knew Himself to be the final Word.

The Old Testament must be known and loved not merely for the sake of understanding the recorded teaching of our Lord, but in order that we may understand what He did not say or is not recorded as having said because it was in the minds and hearts of His hearers, or those to whom His teaching was handed on. His appeal to the Scriptures, God spake unto Moses saying, I am the God of Abraham and the God of Isaac and the God of Jacob; He is not the God of the dead but the God of the living, so tremendously significant in itself, points to a much wider context of teaching on the basis of the common ground of the Old Testament than we can safely ignore. Nor can we forget that Apostolic preaching has for its presupposition a knowledge of the Hebrew Scriptures. Even when St. Paul is writing to churches largely Gentile in character, he can assume upon their part a familiarity with the Old Testament which surprises us until we realize how far-reaching in the ancient world had been the appeal of Jewish teaching concerning the One God. I rehearse these familiar truths only because they warrant the statement that the Old Testament makes its own necessary and distinctive contribution to our knowledge of God. Grant all that may be said about its preparatory character, of the necessity of reading it in the light thrown across its pages by our Lord's fulfilment of its meaning, that preparation has a permanent value of its own. There is a meaning to be fulfilled. The attempt to state these truths may be open to the charge of insufficient appreciation of the New Testament, of failure to read between its lines, for the difference is largely one of emphasis, or that between the explicit and the implicit, but it is dangerous to forget that, in religion, emphasis, proportion, perspective are of the first importance. Indeed, if I mistake not, there are not wanting signs of that loss of perspective which has resulted from the practical neglect in our preaching and teaching of that which the Old Testament has especially to give. Let me take an extreme, but, I think, illuminating illustration.

In his Yale Lectures Dr. Coffin quotes a very frank theological teacher as having confessed to him in a moment of confidence: "I haven't the least difficulty with the divinity of Jesus; He is the God I adore. What I want to be assured of is that there is a divinity like Him in charge of the universe."

It is easy to deplore such a confession as lacking the very fibre of Christian faith, to account for it as the inevitable result of the loss of grip that accompanies theological eclecticism, but one element in the situation certainly is the failure to realize the significance and power of Hebrew monotheism as the foundation of Christianity. It is just the sort of thing that a Greek of the first century might have said. That thoughts like these are in many hearts we may learn from the writings of Mr. Wells. We do ill to let slip from our religious consciousness the vast cosmic range and majesty of Israel's doctrine of God, who taketh up the isles as a very little thing, with whom the nations are as a drop of the bucket, who sitteth upon the circle of the earth, and the inhabitants thereof are as grasshoppers.

Or again, we are for the most part much at ease in Zion. Our religion tends to be a very comfortable thing. The same lecturer says effectively that in much religious intercourse,

> the air
> Nimbly and sweetly recommends itself
> Unto our gentle senses. The heavens' breath
> Smells wooingly here.

I do not forget that the New Testament makes the Cross central, that our Lord's challenge often rings out with a strange sternness, but these come home more surely and compellingly to the heart of him who knows God of the prophets, whose righteousness can be a devouring flame. The love made manifest on the Cross is from the heart of the God who answereth by fire.

Had I time I should like to dwell upon the secularity of the Old Testament, the Divine concern with the fortunes of nations and the rise and fall of kingdoms, history seen in all its chaotic fulness as the working out of the Divine purpose, not denying for a moment that this is to be discerned in the New, but insisting on the greater explicitness and breadth of treatment accorded it in the Old. I should like to dwell too on the robust out-of-doors atmosphere which forms the effective setting for the New Testament concentration on the inner life. I confess to reading St. Paul's account of the hardships he had endured in his missionary journeys with the greater interest because I know that, being a Jew, he found in the marvellous scenery of Asia Minor more than the setting for his own spiritual adventures. The sovereign splendour of God as revealed in the world of nature is assumed in the New Testament, but we cannot afford to ignore the Old Testament witness.

This primary purpose of setting forth the truth about God should determine the method of ordering the reading. Selection is necessary for it is obviously impossible in the course of the Sunday lessons to cover the whole of the Old Testament and it is idle to assume that the congregation is accustomed to attendance upon daily services. But in the course of a year's reading, certainly in two years, if as now a two years' course is projected, a sufficiently varied selection might be made which would be fairly representative of the whole of the Bible. And if we give over the effect to provide a large amount of edifying material from which each hearer may appropriate that which meets his own need, or to entice the interest by the unfolding of a more or less complicated narrative, contenting ourselves with giving in its stark simplicity a single incident or a brief prophetic utterance, we shall discern that, by the way in which it speaks of God, the Old Testament still has power to fix men's minds on that which lies beyond themselves and their own needs. And this look away from self is of the very essence of worship. It is to my mind a happy proposal of the Prayer Book Commission which permits the passing at once to the service of Holy Communion after the canticle which follows the first lesson. It seems to me to provide for just that use of the Old Testament which shall emphasize its place in worship. This would seem to carry with it the further implication that the length of the Old Testament lesson should be not unlike that of the Epistle and Gospel. It would not appear a serious objection that short lessons ask people to get up and down too frequently. It is the relaxation into the softness of the cushions that is too often fatal. Worship may demand some alertness of body as well as soul.

For the daily lessons a similar course might be followed, covering much more ground but keeping the lessons brief. If people get a glimpse of the greatness of the main theme, they may be trusted to look up the context for themselves. If the main theme does not interest them, acquaintance with the context will not be of much value. So much of power is to be found in the world drama so strikingly unfolded that there would be gain here in following the general order of the Bible without however attempting to make the reading continuous. There is place for omissions if the criterion is not too narrowly what we are pleased to call unchristian meaning. Many have more historical sense than we are wont to credit them with and those who use daily lessons may be asked to develop it in the light of their belief in the God of history.

For the Sunday-school—dare one attempt to say anything about so difficult a subject in a paragraph or two? We speak today of the Church-school and it is well if by the Church we mean the worshipping community in which the true life of fellowship is found and developed. Preparation for worship is then its first aim, and for this the knowledge of God is essential. To this as I have tried to show, the Old Testament has its indispensable contribution to make, and it is the main business of the teacher to make this clear. Abraham's venture of faith invests him with a great deal of interest, and the child may be taught to discover the same latent instinct in himself, but it is of more consequence that he should come to learn that Abraham is making answer to the call of God, in order that the child may recognize in his own capacity for self-sacrificing en-

deavour the voice of Another than himself. The pupil misses
the point of the Joseph stories so long as he sees only someone
whose virtues are held up for his imitation and does not mark
such teaching as "God sent me before to preserve you a pos-
terity in the earth and to save your lives by a great deliverance,"
or that given in the simple words, "The Lord was with Joseph."
I am not unaware of the necessity of practical instruction, but
I hold that an hour on Sunday cannot compete with the steady
drift of precept and example by which the child's life is shaped
during the week unless that hour is devoted to such fundamental
teaching as shall provide new vision of the meaning of life as a
whole. It cannot surely be seriously urged that the statement,
God made me and all the world, is a satisfactory substitute for
the first chapter in Genesis. It has its place in a catechism
which presupposes Biblical teaching or is to be supplemented
by it, but as compared with the solemn rhythmic splendour of
Genesis its compact brevity suggests a tidy little world ill-
fitted to withstand the shock of actual life and its egocentric
implication—me nicely balanced between God and the world—
taken alone, is rather appalling.

The child will ask questions, and the teacher will have difficulty in answering them, but that would seem to be part of the
business of teaching. After all, the simple dogmatic inculcation
of truth is not the whole of education. The spiritual imagination
of the child must be accorded its rights, and the Old Testament
rightly taught will open a land of far distances where reigns the
King in His beauty and sovereign power.

It means of course that the teacher must understand, and
it is to be feared that at present he does not. He is bewildered
by the confusion into which criticism has thrown him, in which
we most of us share. Our eyes have been intent on externals,
the conditions under which the process was shaped. In the
first flush of enthusiasm over evolution the environment
seemed to be the ruling factor. Now it has been realized that
after all there is a strange, unceasingly urgent power that sub-
dues environment and triumphs over it, moulding conditions
as much as, if not more than, it is itself moulded by them—

nothing other than life. So it is the unceasing power of God Himself shaping and purifying life, making it all the vehicle of His purpose, that we shall again feel to be the really significant element in the Old Testament, and once again we shall declare with unfaltering conviction that this is indeed His Word. Then perhaps instead of thinking of reducing our liturgical reading to the level of our preaching we shall set our preaching of the Old Testament in some adequate relation to our reading, and so declare the whole counsel of God.

SHALL WE RETAIN THE OLD TESTAMENT IN THE LECTIONARY AND SUNDAY SCHOOL?

By Wilbur Larremore Caswell

IT may not be entirely superfluous to note the exact limits of our question, which is fairly narrow in its scope. It does not ask whether the Church Congress shall abolish the Old Testament, and officially declare it not to have been written; it does not propose to banish it from the curriculum of the seminary, or the study of the clergyman; nor does it ask whether we should violently snatch it from the hands of the inquiring and studious layman. It asks whether, in its present liturgical and pedagogical use, it fulfills a real purpose.

Surely it need not be established that a knowledge of the Old Testament background is essential to one who would preach the Christian Gospel. The Old Testament is a vital part of the world's spiritual heritage, the record of God's revelation of Truth to that people whom He had specially prepared to receive it, the account of the spiritual aspirations which found their complete answer in the Incarnation. All this is obvious, but it does not answer our question. The preacher of the Gospel should know Greek, and should study homiletics, but he need not read them in church and teach them. The average worshipper and Church-school student is not a trained thinker or a thorough student of religion. We must impart the Gospel to him in an hour or less each week, with most of the other hours, theoretically and practically, working against us. The question perhaps is, Have we time for the Old Testament?

In stating the problem, I assume: (1) that it is the supreme duty of the Church to teach the Gospel of the Incarnation, and to select, arrange, and reject material, from the Bible and elsewhere, with that sole end in view; (2) that practically, if not officially, this Church has adopted the modern critical view of the Old Testament. It is taught in our Seminaries, and accepted by most of the clergy. We also believe, perhaps as a corollary, that while God's Revelation to the Jews was the most important, it was not the only preparation for the Incarnation. Indeed, some of the Old Testament prophets prepare us for some such broad view of God's dealings with man.

Most of us accept these two propositions, but we read and teach the Old Testament as if we still held that pious view of apostolic succession which fixed the foundation of the Church at God's Covenant with Abraham, or was it Noah, or perhaps Adam? We do not preach as if we held that view. It may be that our preaching is wrong. But if the emphasis of our sermons is correct, our Lectionary and School lessons are hopelessly wrong, for we teach in the latter what we deny or ignore in the former.

If it is agreed that our chief business is to teach the Christian Gospel to the Twentieth Century, which has not much time to listen; that the Old Testament is naturally not Christian; that our religion is not the Bible, the whole Bible, and the Bible only, may we not ask whether the burden of proof is not really on the Old Testament, to show cause why it should be granted a place in an uncongenial atmosphere?

All the possible reasons for the use of the Old Testament may be summed up under two general purposes,—edification which is obvious in the lessons themselves, and a knowledge of Christianity through a study of how it came about.

I fear that the preacher greatly exaggerates the number of Old Testament lessons which are edifying in themselves. To avoid serious misunderstanding most of them require explanation, expurgation, and evasion, which practically amount to denaturisation. The preacher is deceived by his love of good texts and dramatic situations. The Old Testament is full of good texts, but often they occur in chapters which we would not read as lessons. Texts from the Psalms, unsurpassed in spiritual depth, are crowded between imprecations which have no place in the Christian vocabulary.   Some of the most inspired passages in the prophets occur in the midst of material which the average hearer simply cannot understand, and the clergyman often cannot unless he comes into the service fresh from a commentary. We delight in reading the Song of Deborah, and in preaching a sermon on "Curse ye Meroz! Curse ye bitterly the inhabitants thereof; because they came not to the help of the Lord, to the help of the Lord against the mighty." Let us continue to preach from that stirring text.   But why read the lesson? The sermon usually deals very lightly with the actual events which Deborah celebrates, and is concerned chiefly with the lost opportunities of our hearers.   And they are not, like the preacher, on a ceaseless scent for spiritual applications, but will be most impressed with the resemblance between the story and the instructions of the German General Staff.   The story of Elijah on Mount Carmel is a dramatic masterpiece, and it too contains a good text; but its entire point is one we have continually to deny.   The god that answers by fire is not always the God we ought to choose.

From this point of view,—the edification in the lessons themselves,—we might divide our Old Testament material into that which is (1) actually helpful to the average person who takes it literally, and sees only what is there, (2) harmless, and irrelevant to our purpose, (3) harmless, and tiresome, (4) a hindrance to the teaching of the Gospel.   I think there can be no doubt that the first of these classes would prove by far the smallest.

Consider, for instance, the first chapter in the Bible, commonly used to teach the first lesson a Christian child should learn,—that God made him, and all things, and loves and cares for him.   Frankly, should we ever think of using the Creation Story if it were not forced into our hands? We have all attempted to teach it, with one anxious eye upon the biology which will soon come in school, and the other eye upon our traditional reverence for the story as a part of Holy Writ. We explain that the Bible makes no claim to teach science, but that this beautiful story is written solely to remind us that in the beginning was God. But then why teach anything beyond the first verse? We show that for its time this story was the most inspired account of the origin of the world. But our children may remind us that they are living now, and,—as one little girl of eight actually did reply,—that there is a far better account of the Creation in the Child's Book of Knowledge. It is absurd to call the Creation Story poetry. It is primitive science, as exact as a geological chart. But it is not correct science. Does it add anything to the simple statement, "God made me and all the world," except a serious stumbling-block to faith?

How much in the lives of the Patriarchs is edifying to the unhomiletical mind? Certainly the Call of Abraham is a spiritual fact of momentous importance, God's first revelation of a fundamental Christian conception,—the doctrine of election. But has not this idea become common property, a part of the Christian dialect we all speak? Are we not all perfectly familiar with the fact that God chooses men and nations to work out His own purposes? Need we be continually delving after the roots of that notion? Is there very much else of importance in the details of Abraham's life? The story of Joseph I should classify as "harmless, and irrelevant." Children enjoy it; but just what of spiritual value do they get from it? Perhaps the events in Joseph's life were providentially arranged to provide us with a type of the life of Christ. If that is true, and the lessons are read for that purpose, the matter is worth at least one sermon. But who has, within the past twenty years, devoted a sermon to Joseph as a type of Christ?

The life of Moses contains much, of course, of great spiritual value, but should we not have to classify most of Leviticus and Numbers as "harmless and tiresome?" The story of David and Goliath, as few other stories in the Old Testament, teaches its own lesson,—the age-old truth that God chooses the weak to confound the mighty. But, except his encounter with Nathan, is there much else in the life of David which can be trusted to teach an important lesson and raise no troublesome problems?

It is true that Prof. G. Stanley Hall, in his famous book on

Adolescence, asserts that the Old Testament stories are admirably adapted to the needs of childhood, fitting perfectly into his theory of the various stages of development. It is the fashion to accept Stanley Hall's word as law, but might one venture to suggest that he is greatly interested in the periods of child life, and not at all in the Christian Creed? He would teach cave-man religion to the boy at the cave-man stage. When the child prays, "O God, give me a base-ball, and I will go to Church," he would hand him the story of Jacob's bargain with God. The child could perfectly understand and sympathize with Jacob, but is it right at any stage to teach a child to pray as Jacob prayed? Must not the Church bring Jesus Christ and His God in some way to even the youngest child?

There is much teaching that might well be called Christian in the Prophets and the Book of Job. But these books can hardly be taught successfully in any but the advanced classes of the Church School, and mere reading in Church can never get the profound spiritual truths into the minds of the congregation. The important passages need to be sifted out from much that is unintelligible, and even then their message is not perfectly clear without much explanation. The Book of Job expounds a Christian truth contrary to much of the teaching of the rest of the Old Testament,—that we cannot now discover any fixed relation between suffering and sin. Yet is it not true that any intelligent preacher could drive that lesson home to the average mind more effectually by fifteen minutes' explanation than by advising the reading of the entire book, or the listening to it in church?

To all this it may well be said that we can hardly expect the Old Testament to teach Christianity. But we are here for no other purpose.

Perhaps most of the arguments for the use of the Old Testament are of the second sort I have mentioned,—those which suggest the teaching of Christianity through a knowledge of how it came about. Every Christian ought to be familiar with the long process of Revelation. He should know how God prepared the way for the Messiah, and how the Incarnation is

the climax of unmeasured ages of spiritual striving.   Because
the Incarnate God was born a Jew, and proclaimed Himself the
fulfillment of the Jewish prophecies, the Old Testament becomes
a vital part of the Christian Faith.

This is doubtless true for the student, clergyman or layman,
but is it necessarily true for the average Christian with whom we
must do quickly what we have to do?   Just how will it help him
to proceed to the Incarnation by way of Abraham, Isaac, and
Jacob?

A missionary in China once made the rather novel suggestion
that for the Chinese, instead of the Hebrew Old Testament,
selections from their own religious books should be bound up
with the New Testament.   It did not seem necessary to him to
drag the Chinese through the crudities of an alien civilization
before leading them to Christ.   And this, after all, was simply
the method of St. Paul at Athens.   It was also the method of
the Church in formulating her Creeds.   She put them into
Greek, not Hebrew, terms.

Why does the same principle not apply to modern Americans?   St. Paul explained the Cross through the Hebrew sacrifices.   But those sacrifices have to be explained to us.   He
commended the Incarnate Christ to them through their hope of a
Messiah.   But what place has that hope in our own thought?
The Cross of Christ is infinitely greater than any Jewish theory
of Atonement, and we to-day can make it far more real through
illustrations from modern life than through these sacrifices,
and the Jewish theory concerning them.   And the Incarnation
is greater than any Hebrew conception of the Messiah.   Why
not get at these Christian doctrines directly, without all manner
of explanations and figures which themselves need to be explained?

Analogy is always dangerous, but imagine for a moment that
we applied our present use of the Old Testament to the teaching
of Civics and Hygiene in the schools.   The average child does
not remain in school beyond the age of fourteen, and these
subjects must be taught concisely and effectively.   To give
the young child a broad view of civics, shall we start with

primitive society, and discuss the very beginnings of government, considering at some length the failures of the Greek republics, and the development of the English Parliamentary system, thus fitting the child to understand the government of America? Or shall we begin with the Declaration of Independence and the Constitution, teach them the American ideals, and their duty to try to live up to them? In teaching hygiene, shall we begin at once with the theory of germs and the use of soap and the toothbrush, or shall we first ask the pupils to commit to memory the prescriptions and incantations of the medicine-men, teach them in great detail the methods of torture practiced by medieval physicians, and thus lead them to a more thorough understanding of the real meaning of germs and a deeper insight into the use of the tooth-brush? Civics and hygiene, it is true, are not the Revelation of God. Yet to the student of Civics, every movement towards good government, to the student of hygiene, every manifestation of the scientific spirit, is as holy a thing as is each stage of God's Revelation to the theologian. If this method would be utterly absurd in the one case, bewildering the children, and almost defeating its own object, why does it not require considerable defense in the other?

And if all the stages of Hebrew religion which prepared the way for the Incarnation are a vital and necessary part of Christianity, what of the stages of Greek thought which led up to the Nicene Creed? If to understand and properly to worship Christ, the Jewish Messiah, one must know the Old Testament, why, to worship properly the Christ of the Nicene Creed, must one not be familiar with the development of Greek philosophy? For surely the Christ of the Nicene Creed has as many points of contact with Greek philosophy as with Old Testament theology. Why not, then, include Plato and Plotinus in our Lectionary and School curriculum?

Is there not a real danger, in our emphasis on the Old Testament, of making our Lord the Hebrew Messiah, rather than the Universal Christ, and perhaps teaching a religion and ethics of a Judaised type? For after all, the Old Testament, whatever it should have done, did not lead the Jewish people to Christ, and St. Paul definitely broke with the spirit of the Old Testament. God is not the God of the Hebrews only, and we must present Him, not in Hebrew, not in Greek terms, but in terms of our own life and thought. This the Church has done in her best days, Some of her most fixed formulas and unvarying customs had their origin in this thorough-going modernism. Can we not find a Christ for this age, without leading our people around a loop of some thousand years? We have our own background of Christian thought, Christian concepts which have been in the air for many centuries, and it seems hardly necessary to work our way up to them again and again through Jewish theology.

But just what shall we do with the Old Testament?

I venture to ask whether we must not have some sort of shorter Bible, a very much shorter Bible, containing only such passages as the average person might be supposed to comprehend, and with nothing that actually hinders a true conception of Christianity. Could not the First Lesson at Morning and Evening Prayer be optional, or at least composed of a few short selections, the grand old passages which might well be heard many times in the course of the year? If there should be any attempt to demonstrate a religious development, or to show "the difference Christ has made," this should be clearly indicated in a title or preface, for the worshipper has a perfect right to suppose that whatever is read to him in the Church service is a message from God, and to be accepted as true.

And in the Church-school, could not the Old Testament as a whole be taught only in advanced classes, and in the regular course a series of lessons, along the lines of the Christian Nurture Old Testament stories, but far more drastic, which give merely the great facts concerning the important Old Testament characters? In many cases, but one event would suffice, in order that the pupils need not be deprived of those names which are dim but majestic symbols of noble ideals, or perhaps edifying illustrations of great sins. But we cannot teach the evolution of religious ideas to the young. They accept all that is taught as equally true, and they ask, in the words of a little girl in my own School, "Why do you make us learn all about Abraham, Isaac, and Jacob, and then tell us that they were not good Christians, and that their God was not quite like our God?"

How seriously should we suffer if such a change were made? Have the worshippers in other Communions, who seldom hear the Old Testament read in their services, any less worthy or complete an idea of God than our people? Are the children of the Roman Catholic Church any worse Christians because the Old Testament is largely neglected?

Some change is essential, and no lectionary or system of lessons has really met the issue. If in theory there are some which are admirably calculated, according to psychological and pedagogical principles, to lead hearer or pupil to a clear conception of the Christian Gospel, the reply is that, practically, they do not.

PART III

THE OBLIGATION OF THE CHURCH TO SUP-
PORT A LEAGUE OF NATIONS

THE OPPORTUNITIES OF THE CHRISTIAN CHURCH UNDER A LEAGUE OF NATIONS

By Howard Crosby Butler

WHEN it was first suggested to me that I accept the honour of addressing the Church Congress at this time, it was proposed that I speak upon a theme the title of which was phrased somewhat differently from the form in which it appears upon the programme as the topic of the evening. The topic originally suggested was The Opportunities of the Christian Church under a League of Nations. By the programme I am scheduled, with two very distinguished speakers to follow me, to speak on The Obligation of the Church to Support a League of Nations. On the former theme, I felt that I might be able to present to you some observations gleaned from long experience and sometime residence in the Near East where the opportunities of the Church are great and promising; on the subject printed in the programme before you, I should hesitate to speak at this time because I realize that there are many in this audience far better qualified to approach it than I am. I communicated with your Secretary on this matter, and the Committee kindly relieved my embarrassment by granting me permission to speak upon the topic originally suggested, for the reason, no doubt, that the subject of The Opportunities of the Church under a League of Nations might be accepted as an appropriate introduction to the Obligations of the Church to support such a league.

If it can be shown that the League of Nations now in process of erection is to be so designed that it will tend to increase the growth and influence of the Church, and, what is more important, will enlarge her opportunities for doing good to the world, then there can be no question of her obligation to support it.

Let us assume that the foundation principle of the League of Nations is the idea of promoting Peace on Earth Among Men of Good Will—I use here the old Catholic interpretation of the text as opposed to that of King James' version, for the reason that I believe there never can be peace among men who are not men of good will.—If this general assumption be true, the Church has good reason to support the League even if there were no other grounds of support.

And I assume that one of the reasons of next importance for the existence of the League is the protection and development of the weaker nations, especially those newly established nations, which are gaining freedom from old tyrannies as the result of the World War. It is evident that some of these new nations (the more highly developed ones) will take their places at once among the independent States. It is equally plain that others of them (the more backward ones) will be obliged for a time to accept guidance and assistance from the older and stronger nations, while others are to remain protectorates in the old sense of the word.

But it would seem that all are to be bound together by the League, either as full members of it, or as represented by their mandataries or protectors. This must mean that the affairs of these smaller and weaker nations are to be administered—or at least guided—by the various members of the League. If these methods and ideals are to be clean and high, there is no question of the Church's duty. If, on the other hand, there is a suspicion that they may be otherwise, the Church has a mighty task to perform in seeing to it that they are altered to conform to Christian ideals, whether, in the mean time, they support the League or not. For, as I shall endeavour to show later, the Church's opportunity in this matter is twofold, on the one hand to help the poor and weak nations through her own ministrations; on the other, to keep watch at home, and see to it that the officials appointed to perform the major and minor tasks of the League in its attempts to assist the weaker nations shall be men whose character and ideals entitle them to bear so great a burden of responsibility.

This is one of the reasons that I, unlike many of my countrymen, welcome the notion of America's assuming the burden of responsibility for one or more of the weaker States, because I feel that we have men (especially of the younger generation) who could, and would, take up that burden, and bear it with credit to themselves and to their country. But someone will say, "Yes, if we could be assured that the type of man you have in mind would be chosen." I believe that the Christian Church has it in her power to insist upon good choices for such responsible positions, if only she could be made to feel her own strength, if only the Christian Church would present a solid front to the world, especially the world as represented in politics. All this is by way of generalization.

Now I wish to consider a few points which have to do with some of these weaker nations, which we believe the League of Nations is intended to champion. The peoples in whose case I am particularly interested, and with whose conditions I am best acquainted, are those who for centuries have been subject to the tyranny of the Turkish Empire, peoples inhabiting the land of our Lord's birth, the cradleland of Christianity, the land of the Seven Churches, and the lands of the Old Testament—Palestine, Syria, Arabia, Asia Minor, Mesopotamia, and Egypt, lands which have given us all that we hold most dear in our religion, but which themselves have profited by Christianity, less perhaps than the frozen North. We can not know as yet just what the disposition of these lands will be, but almost any change would be for the better. We hear of proposals for an independent Armenia, an independent Syria, an independent Arabia, each probably with its friendly guide or mandatary. We hear of Mesopotamia under a protectorate, we hear of a much reduced and humbled Turkey confined to Anatolia, as a protectorate, or under a mandatary, or enjoying complete independence, but in any case closely watched by the League. It can not be that the opportunities of the Christian Church will be otherwise than enlarged and extended under any new governments which the League of Nations may devise for those countries. I know well what the Christian Church has endeavoured to do for these lands during more than half a century, I know what marvels for the betterment of conditions she has accomplished through her hospitals, her schools, and her missionary activities, and I know well the enormous difficulties she has surmounted in accomplishing these marvels, yet I know equally well that she is far from satisfied with what she has done, admirable as it is. Every one of the glorious spirits, past and present, who has been associated with the Church's work in these lands would admit that far more has been accomplished for the physical (and perhaps the moral) than for the spiritual well-being of these peoples. Perhaps this is as it should be, perhaps it is best to begin with the material, or physical, and then take up the spiritual. There is much to be said in favour of this point of view; but I am sure that no missionary would be willing to stop with the one, or to admit that the other was not really the more important.

I fully recognize the difficulties which a fanatical Moslem government has opposed to the progress of Christian missionary endeavour, even to schools and hospitals. I fully recognize the obstacles that are inherent in the jealousies and strifes between the native Christian sects, and their suspicion of foreign Christian work; but I do not despair of a glorious future for the activities of the Church in these lands, just because I believe that the chief hindrance will be removed when the arbitrary power of a fanatical government is restrained, and secondly because I have confidence in the native common sense and amendable character, not only of the Arabs, both Christian and Moslem, but also of the Turkish farmer class.

It is hardly necessary to explain to this audience that the population of what was Turkey in Asia is much divided religiously; that all the Turks and a large majority of the Arabs are Moslems; that the Armenians, in Northeastern Asia Minor, are Christians, and that there are large, though minority, populations of Christians of Arab blood in Syria, Mesopotamia, and Egypt, as well as Christian Greeks in Asia Minor and elsewhere.

Nor is it necessary to explain that these native Christians are divided into many rival, and often hostile, sects—Greek Orthodox, Greek Catholic, Roman Catholic, Syrian, Chaldaean, Maronite, Armenian, Copt, etc. There are also considerable communities which are neither Christian nor Moslem, except in so far as they find it convenient outwardly to profess Islam, such as the Druses, the Nosairiyeh, Kisilbash, etc. No more difficult field has ever been offered to the activities of the Christian Church, yet this should make the work the more stimulating.

The grave question is how to approach the task. Attempts have been made by wiser heads than mine to answer this question; but no satisfactory solution has yet been reached. I know I am stumbling in where Councils and Foreign Mission Boards quite fear to tread, and I do not presume to offer a final solution. But, as a layman, who has covered great stretches of these lands, mile by mile, who has visited many communities never reached by a missionary, who has formed close friendships with natives of all grades and sects, who has employed hundreds of natives in different capacities, and who has known the fallow soil, as well as the soil tilled by missionary effort of all sects, and denominations, I shall here attempt, in all humility, and without intention of criticising the self-sacrificing work of priests or preachers, to offer a layman's suggestions.

The first consideration, as it seems to me, should be the complete reorganization and amplification of the training given to the men and women who are sent out to carry on the Church's work. Heroic zeal has done great things, and will continue to do them; but a very special training added to that zeal will make it 100% more effective. It has long been assumed that a good general education plus a theological course, or perhaps a course in "field work," is sufficient equipment for the worker in the foreign field. To this often has been added a fairly good training in the first principles of medicine. There have been many cases in which this sort of schooling, given to a man of special aptitude for the work, has produced a most efficient worker; but experience has shown that in a much larger number of cases, this training is insufficient. It has seemed to me a great injustice to the high spirit and overflowing zeal of a young man who would give his life to work in the foreign field, to send him forth insufficiently prepared to meet the great difficulties and responsibilities of his position.

It goes almost without saying that the prospective worker in a foreign field should know at least the rudiments of the language of the people among whom he is to work before he enters upon the field. But it is of the utmost importance that he should have a very thorough education in the history, religions, literatures, traditions, manners, and customs of the people among whom he is to live, if he is to become an accepted member of their society and be in a position to help them. I have met representatives of the Christian Church in Syria and Anatolia, who were more ignorant of the tenets of Islam than many of their Moslem neighbours were of Christianity. I have heard them deliver diatribes against the Koran without ever having looked into the book, and against Moslem social customs which do not exist outside of their own imaginations or their early Sunday-school traditions. Christian teachers often show an amazing ignorance of, or perhaps better, an amazing amount of misinformation about, the various Christian sects of the East, their tenets and their practices.

The Turk and Arab are not stupid: the average mentality of the latter is rather high. There is no place in the world where learning is more reverenced than in the Near East. These peoples have no measure of erudition outside of their own intellectual field, and if they find the Christian teacher ignorant in that, they set him down as a dullard, and his power of doing good is thereby greatly diminished. Moreover it is important that the Church should help these people not to be good Americans or Englishmen or Frenchmen, but good Syrians or Armenians, especially under the League of Nations which is to give them freedom. Their own countries will need their help if they are to grow to independence. It is fruitless, if not wrong, to make the youth of these nations scorn their fathers and mothers, and dispise the pit whence they were digged. The

French schools have been perhaps the chief offenders in this connection, making poor imitations of Frenchmen out of Syrian lads, and the American college in Beirut has been a model for the development of national feeling and national pride in the Syrian youth. But there has been too much essay writing by these boys in our schools, on Martin Luther, Benjamin Franklin, and Abraham Lincoln, and not enough attention has been paid to the noble history and fine literature of their own country.

Then medical training is not carried far enough. There is no key which so easily unlocks the door to the human soul as the power to relieve human physical pain. No man or woman should be permitted to enter upon work in a field where doctors are scarce without a thorough knowledge of the simpler remedies for the most common ailments, and full training in first aid to the injured. If the representatives of the Christian religion, of all grades—priests, preachers, teachers, and Y. M. C. A. workers—sent from the West to the East, can be armed with authentic information touching all phases of Eastern life and thought, they will be more than doubly effective. If they can be armed also with the simpler gifts of healing, no doors will be closed to them. All this means very special training, and considerable time and expense. If the Church cannot persuade the colleges to furnish serious courses in such training, she will be obliged to take it up herself in her schools and seminaries, where to my mind, it does not properly belong.

My next point, I approach with even greater hesitancy; for it is one which might well have taxed the powers of an ancient Council. I refer to the question of Christianity versus Christianity. For in the near East one views the spectacle of a divided Western Christendon proposing to teach a still more bitterly divided Eastern Christendom.

The Moslem world may long remain an unfruitful field for Christian labours, beyond such very definite results as are to be derived from teaching, healing, setting a high moral example, and building up a spirit of charity for the sacred beliefs of others. But the old Christian sects always have been, and are likely long to remain, the field of opportunity for the benevolent labours of the Church. These Oriental Christian Churches require no fundamental changes of creed, but only the elimination of ignorance and superstition, and a more perfect correlation between faith and morals, to make them highly effective spiritually to their adherents.

The situation is an extremely delicate one. It is important in the first place that these sects should not be antagonized by foreign Christian workers. They are very proud of the antiquity of their Churches, and often sensitive to the least hint of criticism. Nothing so quickly breeds hostility toward foreign workers as a want of respect on their part towards the ancient forms of Christian worship. The more learned of these Eastern Christians know that while their ancestors were engaged in profound theological controversies about Eutychianism, or the Patri Passion, ours were hunting half naked, or clothed in skins, through the forests of Northern Europe, and bowing down to wood and stone. To them it seems grotesquely paradoxical that, having them in mind, we should sing, "Shall we whose souls are lighted with wisdom from on high; shall we to souls benighted the lamp of life deny." Although I understand that this grand old hymn has been omitted from many of the later hymnals, I fear that too much of the spirit of these lines has been manifested by western Christians in the East towards the adherents of the oldest Christian sects.

These more intelligent Oriental Christians are frank in admitting that the old Churches have failed to do as much for their adherents as they might have been expected to do, and they agree among themselves that the root of the trouble is *ignorance*. Ignorance is difficult to combat but not incurable, with time, if the proper remedy be applied. Of course the only remedy for ignorance is knowledge, and you say, "How shall they learn without a teacher?" and, "Have we not been doing our best to teach them?" I would suggest that the remedy has as yet not been properly applied, that we have been administering it externally, while an internal application is the only one that will effect a cure. In other words, I believe that the old sects must be reached, so far as possible, from within. And this should be the more easy of accomplishment in view of the *rapprochement* between the Churches of the Anglican Communion and several of the Eastern Churches, like the Orthodox Greek and the Armenian. Far more can be accomplished if our Western teachers can teach from within the native churches rather than in schools and chapels set up outside of, and often apparently in opposition to them. But the results would be even more satisfactory, in time, if the Church will provide free education for the would-be priests of these Oriental Churches, either in seminaries established in their own country, or better still, here, in American colleges and seminaries. A Greek or a Syrian priest educated in America, without having the foundation principles of his faith altered in the smallest degree, on returning to his native land, would never urge his flock not to fight locusts by violence because they are sent of God, but by prayers and processions of icons, yet an American cannot go to one of those communities and urge the futility of processions to the exclusion of more practical and forceful efforts, without incurring the suspicion and displeasure of the whole community.

In this same connection another great field of opportunity lies open to the Church here at home in making special provision for the education and the spiritual welfare of the thousands of Oriental Christians who come to our shores, and who often return home, free from native superstitions, but unfortunately too often devoid of respect for their old native faith. The native priests in the near East often complain that their young men come to this country Christians and return atheists. The Church can do much to correct this, especially among those who are really affiliated with her in one communion, and incidentally can help to improve the old sects from within.

In the third place, I would emphasize the importance of the Church's duty and opportunity in our commercial and official relations with all these weaker nations, which a League of Nations would establish and foster. A dishonest agent of an American firm, who would exploit the peasants, or an American government official of unsavory life and habits, can do much, perhaps unwittingly, to nullify the good work of an American religious teacher. The Church has it in her power to keep a more careful watch over appointments both commercial and official, and can do more to encourage young men of high ideals and sound religious beliefs to take up business or official life among these peoples whom the League of Nations intends to free, and whom the Church hopes to raise to higher standards of living.

In order to take full advantage of these great opportunities it is most important that the Church insist that the whole campaign be based upon *Truth*. It is a great shock to one who has travelled widely, and resided long, in the Near East to hear lectures at home, and to read books, and articles in newspapers (even religious papers) based upon untruths and half truths about the peoples of these lands, their religions, their social customs, or habits, and prepared with the sole purpose of being sensational. I would have the Church bar out all harsh criticisms based upon superficial knowledge, I would have her banish from all libraries over which the Church or churchmen have control, all books which treat of these subjects without authoritative information, and I would have her discountenance the publication, in all religious papers, of articles founded upon lies or half truths. Our criticisms must be based upon the truth if the Church is to do her duty well.

I have travelled much among the Arabs, both Moslem and Christian. I know their faults and their virtues—especially the virtue of consideration for the religious beliefs and the native customs of foreigners. I have lived among the Druses and am well acquained with the sturdy worth of those non-Christian, monogamous "Puritans of the East" among whom prostitution is absolutely unknown, and marital infidelity extremely rare, because punished by death of both parties. I have employed over a thousand Turks, during a period of five years, and have worked with them day after day in the trenches of Sardis, yet, in all that time, I have never known a case of cruelty to children or to animals; I have observed only the kindest treatment of old people (for I employ several octagenarians); I have seen only one fight, and that a fist-fight between two lads of sixteen—such a fight as I could probably find at any time within twenty minutes from this building. Yet these are the terrible and ferocious Turks of whom we have heard so much. I hope to see the political power of Turkey crushed, chiefly because I wish to see the farmer Turk saved from his own rulers. I have high hopes of all these peoples, I even believe that there are some virtues which we may learn from each of them.

The fanaticism of the Moslems towards Christianity, and their hatred of Christians, have been much exaggerated. It exists principally as a political weapon wielded by a Government which has been fanatical for its own base purposes. The rank and file of the people are ignorant and superstitious, not generally fanatical; but when the government chooses to make the issue appear as a religious one, the Moslems naturally take sides with the Moslem government, and then their religious devotion is artifically worked up into fanaticism by special agents who represent Islam as threatened by Christianity. During the past twenty years the persecution and massacres of Armenians have been entirely political agitations instituted by the Government. Christians of other races and creeds in the empire were unmolested, until the recent Balkan wars when the persecution of the Greeks in Asia Minor became also a political measure, and until the World War when all Christians, saving the Germans, who are nominally Christian, were subjected to persecution because they were supposed to be in sympathy with the Allies—which most of them were.

But I have seen Moslems and Christians living together in perfect harmony in almost all parts of the Empire. My Moslem and Christian employees dipped peacefully in the same dish regularly at noon time, and when the persecution and expulsion of the Greeks began in the Spring of 1914, my Moslem neighbours were bitterly opposed to these measures, but powerless to restrain the Government. Of course every community has its bad citizens, like New York's gunmen, who can be counted upon to do dirty work for hire; but, with the Government's power to use religious zeal as a political weapon removed, the situation of the Christians in the Near East will be improved fourfold, and the opportunities of the Church correspondingly increased.

Finally I would urge that the Church discountenance hatred and bitterness as illegal weapons in the campaign, especially since the differences between ourselves and these other peoples are chiefly differences in religion.   We may justly cherish righteous wrath against a Government which has wrought every kind of atrocity upon defenseless subjects, but nothing is more painful than to hear a zealous exponent of Christianity attack some other religion with hatred and spite on his tongue, especially if untruths, even unconscious ones, are added to hate and spite.   Let the church send out her army armed with the panoply described by Saint Paul, equipped with full store of scientific knowledge, but scorning to employ the weapons of evil; bound to win in the great campaign for the good of the world which the changed order of things seems to open to her, and in which we pray the League of Nations will help her to succeed.

THE OBLIGATION OF THE CHURCH TO SUPPORT A LEAGUE OF NATIONS

By Talcott Williams

THE Christian Church has a just, inevitable, and effective sympathy with a League of Nations because Christ, before his Ascension, organized the first international society the world had ever seen or heard proposed. No religious or secular leader had ever proposed that the faith that was in him should be taught to all nations. Hebrew prophets predicted that all nations would seek the God of Israel. No one of them before Jesus of Nazareth the Christ had predicted that the servants of the Messiah would preach the Gospel to all Nations. This command has been followed and one of its fruits is the League of Nations.

Perpetually we limit the work of the Church by its visible membership. The Church is the leaven of Humanity. Leaven merges itself in the whole lump and the bread of peace now becoming the sacramental covenant of nations in a common league to end war through law is the work of the leaven of Christ's teaching taught by His Church. From Him, this great war gained its chrism of unselfish sacrifice, in this war from Him comes the conception of the brotherhood of Humanity and it is his peace which He gives to Man not as the world gives it which is the conscious and unconscious purpose of Christian and non-Christian lands. Every worldly influence of capital, concessions, exploitation, and imperialistic ambition is arrayed against this new covenant sanctified by righteous blood shed on the Calvary of this war, and every Christian principle is in its favour. All the opposition heard in this country is based on selfish considerations and every voice raised in protest pleads that this land shall seek its own good and not another's, and bids it turn aside from the hard path and strait of using its strength to protect weaker lands to the broad and easy road of the selfish enjoyment of its power and its pelf solely for itself, denying responsibility for the world's peace.

These considerations alone are enough to decide the responsibility of the Church of Christ towards the League of Peace. But reasons larger and as cogent exist. The Covenant and League of Peace between self-governing nations brings to a world destiny the political equality, freedom, and self-rule of men. The economical equality, freedom, and self-direction of men and women remains to be won. To the founders of the Church all men and women were equal in their rights and their responsibility. None of his followers was to be a ruler but a servant of others. This is the democratic ideal of all political rule, power held for a season and solely for the public rule and service.

A democratic economy will do the same. Our political freedom and equality has been reached not by levelling down but by levelling up, and the rights English barons sought for themselves in Magna Charta have become the common heritage of the English-speaking folk.

The same forces which brought about this political freedom and equality will bring a like economic freedom. As the political power and rights of a privileged class came to be shared by all, so economic power and right will be shared by all, by levelling up through the diffusion of wealth. We long ago accepted one man one vote as just and indispensable in a political democracy. We shall see through the eyes of those who come after us one family one house as just as indispensable, in a democratic economy.

This has already begun in this country where nine million families own land out of twenty million; and three-quarters of our families own some property. High wages are doing as much. The largest exemption of small incomes and the heaviest taxation of the largest known in any land is diffusing property. The great revenue made possible in this method must not be wasted in war. It must be used to raise the general level of comfort. Rehousing, better education, the adequate care and protection of children and all which will make the life, the education, and the opportunity of the child of the captive in some industrial dungeon as safe as the first born of Pharaoh can not come if war is to lay its heavy economic toll on the future. The Church has too much preached the individual responsibility of wealth and too little the responsibility of the State to bring economic equality and privilege; and the final responsibility of the Church for the support of the League of Nations is that it will permit the use of the taxation created by war for the social advance of nations at peace through a Covenant embracing humanity. Private property will remain, and individual ownership, and personal initiative; but the fruits of these will serve an economic democracy instead of ruling it as in the past.

THE OBLIGATION OF THE CHURCH TO SUPPORT A LEAGUE OF NATIONS

By Roland Cotton Smith

THE sudden stopping of a clock at night is more fearful than the sound of it as it echoes along the vacant hall, because the cessation of sound throws us back upon the unseen, unheard spiritual realities and presences; vague, awful, big with unknown possibilities. We welcome any sound that will bind us to the earth. We have become accustomed in the last five years to the companionship of cannon. Their sound has meant to us the ushering in of liberty, justice, and peace upon the earth, and the sudden ceasing of the sound deprives us of our dependencies, throwing us back upon a vague dread world of the spirit, upon forces uncalculable, and possibilities infinite. No wonder that men in the dark of the world welcome any sound that seems to give assurance of stability and security, and promises the day of liberty and peace. But if we do not carry into the day the forces that the night reveals, and that the sun obscures, we shall enter into an unfruitful and unprofitable day.

With the stopping of the cannon that were to bring us liberty and peace, there comes the new note of a League of Nations which is to carry on the work and aims of the war. Nay more than that; it is to establish liberty and peace without war. No wonder that wearied and bewildered men clutch at the idea and pray for the day of its coming; No wonder that men are asking what the church has to say concerning it. The Church has very much to say concerning it. It has the first and last and the important word to say about it, because the Church is the custodian of the spiritual forces revealed in the night which must be carried on into any profitable day.

There would seem at first but one answer to the question that the Church Congress asks. Is the Church under obligation to support a League of Nations? The answer springs spontaneously from our distracted and expectant hearts. Yes. Not perhaps the League of Nations now under consideration. There may be many differences of opinion about details, but A League of Nations—Yes. When we stop to consider the matter, the answer is not so clear. This League of Nations! It sounds all right, but where is it? What is it? Where did it come from? What treasures are within its walls?

It is like a castle that a pilgrim has dreamed of, who now hears the sound of distant hammers. He starts in the direction of the sound and finds himself surrounded and blinded by mists and miasmas obscuring his vision and blocking his way, which have to be penetrated before he can reach his destination and tell whether it is a castle in the air or built upon the solid rock.

The Pilgrim Church has always dreamed of a League of Nations ever since it had the vision that God has made of one blood all the Nations of the earth. The Church has often had to ask of the different attempts to build a League: Art thou it that should come, or do we have to look for another? And now there is another attempt to build the League, and the Church starts forth expectantly to find out what it is. Long before it reaches the building, it finds itself in a mist of sophistries, breathing a rank miasma of personalties. At the very outset it is met by the question, "If you cannot support this particular league you certainly are in favor of some league, of A League of Nations." Meaning (if it means anything) a League constructed in the same general way, along similar lines, amended to meet the needs and desires of the different nations, but fundamentally the same.

A Kingdom of God on earth that cometh without observation, brought about by man's love to man with peace in his heart, is the one dream and aim of the Church. That is a League of Nations to which the Church for ever moves. Now, here is a proposition to build a league within a league, to realize an ideal within the great ideal; it is a means, not an end. And the Church's answer to the question concerning any league of nations that can possibly be secured on the earth today is— Has it within itself the qualities and elements that can help to build the Kingdom of God on the earth? And so the Church says to the sophistry, We will answer the question of a league of nations, when you let us get out of the mists and have a look at the building.

But, cry the voices of the mists, a league of nations is to do away with war; does the Church want war? It is to bring about Peace; does not the Church desire Peace?" and the Church gives answer: The peace that the Church is forever praying and striving for is an entirely different thing from the mere cessation of hostilities! It is the Peace that Christ in the very midst of wars and rumours of wars, said, "I give unto you, not as the world giveth, give I unto you." It is the Peace within the human heart brought about by the victory of the spirit, in the warfare between the spirit and the flesh. Does not the Church hate war? Yes, with all its mind and soul. It is the abomination of desolation, it has the mark of the Beast upon its forehead, but the Church cannot rest there, it is not so easily lulled to a false security. It hears the voice of the Christ crying: "It has been said of old time, Thou shalt not kill, but I say unto you, Whosoever hateth his brother is in danger of hell fire." The Church is infinitely more concerned with hate than with war.

But, say the voices of the mists: A league of nations is to establish liberty on the earth. Do you not want liberty? and the Church replies, We do not want liberty at the expense of truth. It is only truth that will make men free.

Oh, cry the voices of the mists, that is just like the Church. You are always up in the air dealing in generalities and abstract principles. Has not the Church any thing to do with the daily affairs of men. Has it nothing to say to the immediate question to this attempt of man to do something. Why cannot the Church for once come down from the clouds and be practical. Look through the haze of peace and justice and liberty and see how entrancing the building is, as it catches the first beams of the morning sun. Has the Church no sympathy with this effort, no matter how crude it may be to take one practical forward step towards the achieving of an ideal? Oh, why cannot the Church for once be practical. And the church replies, that is precisely what we are, practical! It is you, voices of the mists, who are not practical. You are pronouncing upon the merits of a building before you have reached it, and before you have the slightest idea what the building contains. You are gazing at a light through an atmosphere of fog. And you do not know whether it is a railway signal or a star. The Church is so unreasonably practical that it demands to see a building before it pronounces upon its merits. Why, says the Church to the voices of the mists, why do you detain us here? Why do you not let us go and study this league of nations so that we may find out the worth of it. We do want safety, but not at the expense of salvation. "Safety first" is a good railroad sign to protect the bodies of men, but a poor sign on the road of life to save men's souls. We do want liberty, but we want to know how much of our freedom we will have to pay for it. We *are* crying out for the light of peace, but we want to know whether it is the red light of a traffic regulation, or the star of Bethlehem.

When the Pilgrim Church is fortunate enough to penetrate the mists of casuistry it starts out to find the castle, but before it gets anywhere near the tracks of the league of nations it finds itself breathing a rank and poisonous miasma of personalities. What does a League of Nations involve? What are its bearings and its tendencies? And the Church is surrounded not with lies that might be rejected but with truth that will not be accepted because uttered by persons who happen to be on the other side. Wrong motives are ascribed, false inferences are drawn, and the truth lies buried deep down beneath the prejudices and hates. If the Senators speak, they are playing the game political and hate the President. Well, what of it? Is there any truth in what they have to say? Then seize it from whatever source it comes. The President speaks, and he wants to be the head of the League; well, what of that! does he speak truth or falsehood? That is the vital thing. And we are face to face with this amazing and deplorable fact that the liberty of prophesying is disappearing, and freedom of speech languishes upon the earth. The people who are endeavouring to build a league to establish freedom are by their prejudices and hates killing out all love of truth and fair play, which alone can make men free. We are trying to make freedom live by killing it, and the first task for the Church, before it pronounces upon any league of nations is to burn away the rank miasmas of personalities, with its suffocating prejudices and hates that murder freedom and bury truth and is of far more danger to the people of the world than the rise or fall of any League of Nations.

When the Church has penetrated the mists of sophistries that obscure truth and has passed through the miasmas of personalities that poison freedom, it is in a position to study the idea of a League of Nations and state what its attitude towards it ought to be.

The authorities of the Church Congress, with a leaning towards mercy, made the topic for discussion, "The Obligation of the Church to Support a League of Nations." And that fortunately removes out attention from any particular form and throws us back upon the general underlying principle. We must therefore approach this present proposed form, not to criticise its details, but in order to determine upon what principle of life it is founded. For there are two great opposing principles of life. One starts from the outside and works inward—the other starts from the inside and works outward, inner ever moving outward. One starts with the expression of life to produce life, the other starts with life to produce the expression. One begins with the material to bring forth the spirit, the other begins with the spirit to create the material. One makes good laws to make men good, the other makes men good to make good laws. One would build a cathedral to make men pious, the other would make men pious in order to build a cathedral. One would start with the world to bring about the kingdom of heaven, the other starts with the kingdom of heaven to build a new world. The one is the world method and the other is the Christ method

—the first method is quick, dramatic, and inevitably doomed. The second method is slow and disappointing and eternally triumphant.

> Oh if we draw a circle premature,
>   Heedless of far gain,
> Greedy for quick returns of profit, sure
>   Bad is our bargain!
> Was it not great? Did not he throw on God,
>   (He loves the burthen)—
> God's task to make the heavenly period
>   Perfect the earthen?
> That low man seeks a little thing to do,
>   Sees it and does it:
> This high man, with a great thing to pursue,
>   Dies ere he knows it.
> That low man goes on adding one to one,
>   His hundred's soon hit:
> This high man, aiming at a million,
>   Misses an unit
> That, has the world here—should he need the next,
>   Let the world mind him!
> This, throws himself on God, and unperplexed
>   Seeking shall find him.

These are the two opposing principles. Outward to the inward, or inward to the outward, developing on the one hand, a quick and ineffective method, and on the other hand one that is slow, sure, and eternal! One is the world method, and the other is the Christ Method, and the Church is committed without any reservation to the Christ principle and the Christ method. It is the golden reed placed in her hand to measure temples and cities and kingdoms and leagues. When the church starts with her reed to measure a proposed league of nations, it finds that the purpose of a League is to do away with wars, and to bring peace upon the earth, and to draw nations together. But the moment that the reed touches the idea, it becomes aware of antagonism; the divine reed recoils from the opposing principle. And the church finds that this league is beginning at the wrong end. It begins with an outward association to bring about an inner peace, instead of beginning with an inner peace that will of itself build a league. The nations are not to be bound together by a mutual love of a real peace but by the common fear of horrible war. If the Peace that the league is to enforce or bring about is the mere cessation of hostilities, with the hates and the wars within the natures of men untouched, then the Church has little to do with that kind of peace. A league of nations of that kind is a part of the police regulations of the world—to keep the people in order until they become moral; necessary perhaps; certainly a temporary expedient, playing on the outside of things, leaving the depths untouched. If a league of nations is a police regulation, the Church if it wants to, may commend it as it would commend a policeman, but that is not at all the special work that the Church is placed in the world to do. If on the other hand, the peace that the league is to bring about is the real eternal peace in the human heart, the nations of the world bound together by love, then the Church says to the League of Nations, You never will do it, you never can do it, for you are beginning at the wrong end. You are beginning with the expression of the life instead of beginning with life. But is not one step better than no step at all? And the Church answers, No, for it is a step in the wrong direction. The trouble with the whole matter is that we have taken what may be for the present a good world police regulation and have dressed it up in Christian idealism. When in reality the purpose of a league of nations and the purpose of Christianity are as wide apart as the poles; the dress will not fit. The League of Nations must be stripped of its borrowed idealism, and judged for what it really is—a police regulation to keep a distracted world in order, with the full understanding of the price the world has to pay for it—the curtailment of national liberty; the danger to national independence and the discouragement of free peoples to assert themselves in the future as they have done so gloriously in the past. The order and security of the world just now may or may not be worth the price. But the Church does not have to decide that question. The state has that in hand, for the Church with its golden reed has touched the illusion of what appeared an angel's wings. And so the wings disappear and it discovers a policeman. The Pilgrim Church does not fault the proposed edifice of a League of Nations because it is a castle in the air, but because it is too firmly rooted in the earth. It grows out of the earth instead of coming down from God out of heaven. It does not hitch its wagon to the star, it puts all of its little stars into a wagon, and the wagon carries the star.

The kingdom of the world which begins with the outside of things and starts to bring about Peace by forming a league and the kingdom of Christ which begins without observation in the hearts of men, and starts to build a league by establishing an inner peace; these two kingdoms have ever been opposed. The beginning of the first kingdom was in Babel where the people, essentially one, cried out, Go to, let us build a tower rooted firmly in the earth, which will reach the very heavens. That was idealism, was it not, to reach the heaven? It was good, was it not, to take one step at a time, a thousand feet this year and a thousand feet the next? But God came down to look at the tower, and saw that it was beginning at the wrong end. And His spirit went out of the stones and out of the hearts of men who built the stones, and the tower crumbled. And the peoples were scattered in a confusion of tongues. It is all right to build a tower from the earth, only do not clothe it with an idealism it does not possess. Call it by its right name—a watch tower.

This same temptation assailed Jesus, who came down from God out of heaven to establish peace in the hearts of men, to use some quick external method to bind the kingdoms of the world together. And Jesus withstood Satan to his face, and stepped down from the pinnacle of His temptation and entered into His rightful kingdom in the individual hearts of men. And at the very end of His ministry, with wars and rumours of wars all about Him, Jesus came out of His Kingdom, to rebuke the Church with a terrible denunciation of hypocrisy which is nothing more or less than the starting with the outside of things instead of starting with the inside, whether the thing be a cup or a world—the Church, today not owning phylacteries, does not broaden them, and when it takes the cup it scrupulously cleanses the inside of it, and by so doing it thinks that it has escaped the divine denunciation of hypocrisy. But it cannot escape the terrible denunciation hurled upon it if it begins with and depends upon any principle or method that starts with a League to bring about a Peace instead of going down into the heart of man and establishing there an eternal peace that will fashion an eternal League and form the true parliament of nations and the federation of the world. The Pilgrim Church dissolving the mists of sophistries and the miasmas of personalities, stands with its golden reed to measure a league of nations, and stripping it of its borrowed idealism, exposes a watch tower to keep the world in order,—watch tower built on the earth, that will never reach the heavens, to be controlled and regulated by the State. And the Church leaves it as it leaves all legislation and leagues and uniforms and uniformities and goes on to the vision of the new Jerusalem that comes down from God out of heaven to establish freedom and love and peace in the human heart by the service and sacrifice of the individual man. The spiritual Jerusalem that is not in some other world but is built out of the visions and achievement of mankind, in coöperation with God, that stands above every city and every nation and country, Japan and Germany and Italy and France and England and Russia and America, the Jerusalem that is above and is free, and is the mother of us all.

I was given a reed to measure the city, and the length and the breadth and the height of it are equal, and there shall be no more curse and no more war.

> All the peaks soar, but one the rest excels,
> Clouds overcome it:
> No! yonder sparkle is the citadel's
> Circling its summit.
> Thither (the Church's) path lies,
> Wind we up the height.

> Stars come and go! Let joy break
>   with the storm,
>   Peace let the dew send!
> Lofty designs must close in like effects:
>   Still loftier than the world suspects,
> Living and dying.

The League of Nations that the Church endorses is built out of human hearts redeemed by the operation of the law of sacrifice revealed in the shedding of the blood of Jesus Christ.

Inward ever more to outward, built to music. And therefore never built, and therefore—built for ever.

PART IV

ESSENTIALS OF PRAYER BOOK REVISION

ESSENTIALS OF PRAYER BOOK REVISION

By Charles Lewis Slattery

PEOPLE who have used the Prayer Book all their lives are sensitive to any change in it. We are apt to say that if a man desires more modern services, let him have them, but do not let him adapt any Prayer Book service to his present need. We should then keep the Prayer Book for people of long liturgical training, and we might suggest unusual freedom to others. Instantly the book would cease to be a Book of Common Prayer. It would become a book for the initiated who chanced to know beautiful archaic forms and who found the music of ancient words more inspiring than the clearness of modern phrasing. For others some little mission book might be a refuge.

In the past the Prayer Book has been an eloquent inducement to many a reverent person outside the Church to enter into the joy of public worship. We must remember the increasing number of truly religious people who are inclined to be satisfied with private prayer. For their sakes, as well as our own, we cannot allow the book to lose its ancient appeal. Can we not have one book which will satisfy the historic sense and yet seem real to the young and to the stranger? Is there not some way by which all the dignity of the past may be kept, while the Prayer Book services are shaped, by a deft touch here or there, into a form which shall make them the living medium of the best aspiration of our own time? I believe that with patience the old Prayer Book, without losing its flavour, may become such a living book; and so I ask the privilege of pointing out some of the principles which might guide men in making a revision.

I

The first principle is to make liturgical propriety a servant and not a master. It is possible to meet every suggestion for a drastic change with a shrug of the shoulder and the cold comment, "Liturgically incorrect." We must remember that the *Te Deum* was once an innovation, and we can imagine how the faithful at Arles, for instance, complained when, in the fifth century, it began to be used instead of a canticle from Holy Scripture. It was because the *Te Deum* was a superb hymn of faith, not because it was "liturgical" (which people doubtless said it was not) that it won its way. So too it was not till the the eleventh century that the metrical hymn, *Veni, Creator Spiritus*, was introduced into the Ordinal of the Western Church. We feel that it is one of the most sacred parts of an ordination, yet it was not written till the ninth century, and there must have been stormy protests from the conservative when it began to be used. Only the fact that all through the years it has touched the hearts of people, as scarcely anything else in the Ordination Service, has saved it.

Another note of warning is necessary in this connection. The roots of liturgical usage strike down into an exceedingly dim past. When we get beyond a certain period, which is far from early, no one knows much about the exact forms of services which were used. When we find certain features later becoming evident in various parts of the Church we may rightly assume that they point to a common origin, a primitive use. But in general we must be wary of any one who tells us that this or that detail is the invariable custom of the Church from the beginning. Liturgical correctness must be mentioned with humility.

When all this is said, however, there is a sense of liturgical fitness which can be felt rather than defined. This sensibility is a gift something like the gift which enables a critic to tell real poetry or real art. Not many have it. It may or may not come with erudition. It comes, in part at least, from life-long association with some great liturgical use and from an innate reverence. When the people in the Church discover that they need a new way to express their worship, it becomes the duty of those who have the liturgical instinct, to find the form, simple, stately, inevitable, which will make the new an integral part of the old. It has been done again and again in Christian history: it can be done today.

II

Notice, now, some of the demands which the people of today are making upon those who guide public worship. These demands are evident from the experience of those who minister not only in parish churches, but in academic chapels and in soldiers' camps. The most insistent demands come when men are most deeply interested. I may group some of these demands under the head of The Will To Hold The Attention.

(a) Words which need a knowledge of archaic English or difficult theology in order to mean anything to the listener must be translated. When the English Reformers took the service out of an unknown language and put it into the common language of the people they committed the Church to a great principle which must be constantly obeyed. "Prevent," in the sense of "go before," is an archaic word. In 1789 our fathers changed the English collect, "Prevent us, O Lord, in all our doings with thy most gracious favour," to read, "Direct us, O Lord, in all our doings . . . ." We ask why they did not also translate the Collect for the Seventeenth Sunday after Trinity, "Lord, we pray thee that thy grace may always prevent and follow us." Probably they could not find a substitute for "prevent" which was equally mellifluous: one hopes they tried. In any case that task is left to us. The Commission on the Prayer Book will report to the next General Convention a number of more accurate translations for verses in the Psalter which are now wholly unintelligible.

(b) We are discovering that it is not a long service which frets and wears down the attention, but the service wherein there are too long sections of doing only one thing.

The *Te Deum* when sung (as it ought to be) is too long, as a continuous "use," for the interval between the Lessons. It is the time, a little more than occasionally, for a shorter anthem or for a metrical hymn. I am astonished by the number of reverent young people who tell me that the service lags for them at the *Te Deum* even in churches where it is superbly sung. The truth is that the *Te Deum* is a wonderful act of worship in itself and needs space. One cannot fear its neglect through giving permission to exchange it now and then for a shorter canticle, as is now tentatively provided by the last General Convention. And if a metrical hymn like Heber's "Holy, Holy, Holy, Lord God Almighty!" could be included among the alternatives, the gain would be enormous. No real liturgical principle would be sacrificed, and a practical end would be gained. I am sure that if the saints of the fifth or of the eleventh century had possessed such a hymn they would unhesitatingly have incorporated it into their service books. The time will come when we shall have as sound liturgical judgment.

But the chief error is to have prayers too long, or to have too many prayers in one part of the service. The more intense the effort to fill every sentence with a real prayer of the heart, the more distressing is the crowding of words which at last breaks down the ability to pray. The more modern prayers in Morning and Evening Prayer are all too long, as are most of the special prayers and thanksgivings. The concise collect is the form of prayer most likely to inspire the soul to pray. The suggested revision of the prayer for those in affliction takes out all attempt to explain affliction, and tersely asks God for remembrance in mercy, for patience, for comfort, for peace. The mind is filled by the directness of the prayer. It will become more and more a question whether our revision of 1789 really improved the Prayer of Consecration in the Holy Communion. The three prayers added are of profound value yet at a place in the service so intense as this, it may be doubted if we should not be grateful if we could stop with the Invocation.

In the same way the Litany is too long to be said with another service, and when used alone, it ought to be broken by a hymn or hymns. The responsive character of the Litany makes it a valuable help in holding the attention: but permission to use alone sections of the Litany would mean more real worship for most people.

(c) We are discovering that an easy way to hold the attention is to have certain prayers said by the people themselves. Already the General Convention has taken the first step in allowing the General Thanksgiving to be said by the people with the minister. There is no doubt that after a series of prayers to which people have been only listening, this participation reclaims the attention. The Prayer of Humble Access in the Holy Communion would certainly have redoubled force if said by every one. This principle might be extended to some other prayers and thanksgivings for specific occasions. Once the Prayer Book could be read only by a fraction of the congregation. We cannot go on using it as if the majority of us could not read it. The fact that we can all read as well as the minister invites to the thought that in more than one or two places we might join our voices as well as our hearts in supplication.

III

A principle which is thrusting itself upon us is the need of unity in every service. The Revision of the Prayer Book ought not to stop till the service for each Sunday morning, at least, is made into one clear unity, or till, by permission and suggestion, the intelligent minister may so make it.

It is unfortunate that recent General Conventions have committed the revision of the Lectionary to one committee, the revision of the Prayer Book to another; for the Lessons have an intimate relation to the unity which is desirable. Let me give an illustration. There is no one day (if Epiphany is to symbolize only the manifestation of Christ to the Gentiles) when our Lord's Baptism is specifically commemorated. The Prayer Book Commission is therefore suggesting that the Gospel for the Second Sunday after the Epiphany be the account of our

Saviour's Baptism. How marked would the teaching value of this Sunday become if the Psalms, the Lessons, the hymns, and the sermon could all bear upon Baptism! The great days are already unified, but each Sunday ought to be an inspiring unity, both for remembrance and for teaching. The Lessons and the Psalms for Quinquagesima ought to carry forward the thought of the Collect and the Epistle; the First Sunday in Lent ought to have Psalms and Lessons which would teach the victory over temptation; the whole service for the Second Sunday after Easter should lead up to an inevitable sermon on The Good Shepherd.

Incidentally one may say a word about the length of Lessons. We have a fruitful liturgical suggestion in the length of the Epistles and Gospels. Through long experience the Church has found what length of Scripture passage is most conducive to edifying. A whole chapter may or may not give a unity of suggestion. A parable or the account of a single event is the sort of unity which a Lesson should embody. Shorter, more concrete Lessons from the Old Testament would be especially helpful. And since there are only a little more than one hundred passages to be chosen from the whole Old Testament for all the Sundays and greater festivals, there is no reason why a vivid narrative or a stirring exhortation, perfectly clear to the unlearned, may not be found to enforce the teaching, which, so far as one can tell, the Church intends to be stressed on any particular day. Examples of perfect Old Testament Lessons are the account of Abraham's sacrifice of Isaac, on Good Friday, and the account of Elijah's translation, on Ascension-day, David's lament over Absolom and his lament over Saul and Jonathan are marvellous passages, only one of them now assigned to a Sunday Lesson I believe, and that only recently. Passages from the Prophets which can be understood only by scholars ought not to be read on Sunday; but every one can understand, "My beloved hath a vineyard," and, "Comfort ye, comfort ye my people." For the most part the Old Testament Lessons should be the narratives of Jacob, Joseph, Samuel, and David,—which present supreme truths in terms of personality.

IV

The question arises whether the revision of the Prayer Book may proceed only along lines of form, leaving doctrine quite alone. I believe that any revision which is worth attempting will be bound to touch doctrine. In a book so dear to every one, we may rightly ask that no revision be made unless the doctrinal changes involved are such as command the conviction of all of us.

There are some doctrinal changes suggested by the Prayer Book Commission which do have, I believe, practically unanimous approval. The prayer for the sick and the prayer for those in affliction now imply that both sickness and affliction are signs of God's disfavour. Death is assumed to be a "visitation" for the departed, and a punishment for the surviving friends. Without putting any other theory in the place of this grim philosophy, the prayers are made direct and simple petitions for God's help. It seems certain that every one will be grateful for this doctrinal omission.

Again, in the Baptismal Service the philosophy in the Exhortation, by which a slur is cast upon marriage and the birth of children, is omitted. It may be said that all such phrases could be satisfactorily explained. But in a service so tender and appealing there is no place for harsh words which need explanation. Here again I believe every one will say a glad, Ay.

Once more, the Burial Office has been so revised that it will breathe more Christian Comfort, will have less of the stern parts of the Old Testament, and will grant permission to have prayers in which the departed are lovingly remembered. The only reason for hesitation might be the prayers for the departed, but the language is so carefully chosen, God's protecting care is so thoroughly recognized, that even here one may expect practically unanimous approval.

There are other places where I believe the suggestions of the Commission involve doctrines which a majority or a very large group in the Church do not wish to see changed. In a comprehensive Communion it is, generally speaking, wiser not to disturb the relative emphasis which already exists.

Naturally the part of the suggested revision which will be examined with most careful scrutiny is that which has to do with the Holy Communion. No change is likely to be permitted which does not have a sturdy reason behind it, and a reason which will appeal to the whole Church as adequate. There is a genuine need of permission to make the Service sometimes shorter, especially on week days. There are parts of our present Service which are not historically essential to a complete office: these might be made optional by general consent. Because we live in a time when conciseness is a help to concentration, and therefore to reverence and worship, we ought to be extremely careful about any additions, unless they seem of the utmost importance to every one. When changes or additions involve doctrine on which good men within the Church conscientiously differ, we ought to be charitably cautious not to disturb the present joy with which the Service is used by us all.

The most serious suggestions for change in the Holy Communion are the introduction of the *Benedictus qui Venit* before the Prayer of Consecration, and the attaching of the Lord's Prayer to the end of it.

So far as one can discover, the position of the *Benedictus qui Venit*, when used in early times, was immediately before the Communion, and being used in connection with the Bishop's proclamation, "Holy things for holy persons," meant, "Blessed is he who in the Name of the Lord cometh to receive the Body and Blood of Christ." It seemingly was a later development which attached the words to the *Sanctus*. To put them immediately before the Prayer of Consecreation is to suggest that they refer to our Lord's entrance into the Church at this point as once He was so greeted on coming into Jerusalem. If such an interpretation could be separated from the necessary corollary that before this He must have been absent, we might not complain. Certainly there is here encouragement for an inadequate doctrine of the Presence of Christ in the Sacrament which every one who stops to think must wish to avoid. Such devout and learned Sacramentarians as the late Bishop of Salisbury, Dr. John Wordsworth, have made us see afresh now important it is to maintain our confidence in the perpetual nearness of our Master and not to allow any limiting of this reality.

The other change which many earnest people would regret is the taking of the Lord's Prayer from its present place after the Communion. The Reformers put it there evidently with the intention of showing that Communion was always an essential part of the service. Only when the people had obeyed the Lord who said, "Do this in remembrance of me," only when they had received the Sacred Elements, only then had they been bound together into the unity of His Body so that they might make bold to say, "Our Father . . ." The valuable emphasis upon the necessity of receiving the Sacrament is one which many of us think we need to maintain, and the position of the Lord's Prayer in our present service is the outward sign that, having partaken of the Body and Blood of Christ, we are so far one body in Him that we need and desire the opportunity to pray together in the words of His own prayer.

There is no doctrine involved in the removal of the Prayer of Humble Access to a place immediately before the Communion It would gain a certain force there, especially if said by all the people. But there is something to be said for the contention of Dr. Frere, who pleads that the penitential section of the Service (of which the Prayer of Humble Access is certainly a part) should all come before the *Sursum Corda*. He would put this prayer of humility immediately after the Comfortable Words so that from the *Sursum Corda* onwards we should have only words of confidence and great joy. The Reformers were minded to have all the penitential parts before the Prayer of Consecration; it would be in sympathy with their spirit if we followed Dr. Frere's cogent argument.

There is only one other doctrinal change of which I need speak. In Confirmation, the report of the Commission (following largely the first Prayer Book of King Edward VI) recommends that the Bishop, in placing his hands upon the head of the candidate, say, "I confirm thee in the Name of the Father, and of the Son, and of the Holy Ghost." After which he may say the prayer, "Defend, O Lord, this thy Child," over each candidate or over the whole group. This is a departure from primitive use, so far as one can discover it. The essence of Confirmation is the laying on of hands and the prayer for the giving of the Holy Ghost. The fact that Confirmation is the completion of Baptism is certainly no reason for using the same form: not repetition, but addition, is the fundamental idea. As the Church tends to lose its primitive power it tends to escape from the task of praying by slipping into the easier mode of mere announcement. We know, for example, that in the seeking of absolution, prayer was the primitive method; the optative form was later; and the declaratory form was very late. The argument which apparently has most weight is that it is hard for a Bishop when he happens to be confirming a large class to say the beautiful prayer fifty or a hundred times. It is all part of the tendency to be satisfied with general ministrations and to slight the individual. It is an ignominious flight from the pastoral duty, divinely commanded,—the duty of taking pains to do one's very best for the individual soul. Most bishops have small groups to confirm, and the practical difficulty is not conspicuous. But even if it were the rule for bishops everywhere to be confirming hundreds each week, how better could a bishop spend his time than by giving full attention to the individuals of his flock who come seeking a blessing from the Holy Spirit, so that always afterwards the man or the woman should remember, "While the Bishop's hands were on my head, he prayed that I might daily increase in the Holy Spirit more and more until I came to the Everlasting Kingdom." We shall be wise if we pause long before we exchange an apostolic custom for a convenient modern substitute.

V

Let me draw together the principles which I have tried to define in this paper. In general we must be sure that the changes which are made in the Prayer Book are such changes as the people who are in the pews, and also those who ought to be in the pews, consciously or unconsciously, really desire, changes which would make their worship more intense, and which would more swiftly bring them into the awareness of God's Presence. The academic mind which is interested in quaint phrases or picturesque customs, pertaining to remote places or remote ages, must beware lest it plead for something which is not capable of holding the worship of average people in our own land and our own time. We must cling to the fact that ours is a Book of Common Prayer, a book which shall appeal to all sorts of people now.

Nevertheless the academic mind has its full function in the reconstruction of the book. The historical and the liturgical scholar has a highly important verdict to pass upon the practical requests of those who are face to face with congregations in cities and villages and missionary stations. The scholar must find a form into which the aspiration of the time may be put, so simple that every child will know what is meant, so dignified that Cranmer would think that the English was his own. Through the scholars, the book, which others might make only the book of the age, may be kept the book of the ages.

But scholars are apt to be cautious, as the practical people are apt to be rash. So we must pray for the genius, the poet, the mystic, who will have patience to listen to the longing voices of the time, who will have courage to believe that words can be found to express what God longs to hear from them, and who will have the divinely given power to create a new form here, a new form there, the golden bowls full of incense, which are the prayers of the saints of our own generation.

As the Church is a living Church, so the Prayer Book is a living book. It will never be finished because the Church will grow to need an always greater book. And by God's grace it shall have it.

THE ESSENTIALS IN PRAYER BOOK REVISION

By JOHN WALLACE SUTER

THE outstanding fact about the essentials in Prayer Book revision is that whereas a generation ago they were commonly expressed in negative terms, today the terms of expression are positive. Indeed, up to a very recent date, the mind of the Church in general, in the face of proposals for Prayer Book revision, sought negative expression. The watchwords were two: the first sprang out of a satisfied conservatism which felt that the Book was a very nearly perfect medium for the worship of the people, or for the fostering and sanctifying of Christian life. This watchword was, "Don't touch the precious Book." There was acknowledgment that there might be need of minor corrections, which would concern themselves with moods and tenses and commas, but that nothing ought to be done which could be noticed as change. This feeling was widespread. The people who gave expression to their apprehension when revision was mentioned were, for the most part, older people who loved the Church and her services, and who were faithful, devout and generous adherents, many of whom had come into the joys and satisfactions of Prayer Book worship from experiences in various forms of Protestantism, to which they looked back with a happy sense of release. The worship as embodied in the Prayer Book, just as it stood, had been to them an emancipation and a revelation. They could not bear the thought that the Prayer Book might in any way suffer alteration.

The other watchword which expressed negatively an essential in the matter of revision ran something in this fashion, "Dotn' touch anything in the Book which concerns doctrine, lest the faith be imperilled." The frame of mind expressed in this exhortation is distinguishable from the sheer conservatism of which we have just spoken. It was rather a cry of timidity; there was a genuine fear lest if any changes were made at all in the Book of Common Prayer, it might happen, even without intention, that somehow inadvertently the bulwarks would be weakened and the faith subtly undermined. A great deal used to be said and written about the fact that the Book of Common Prayer was the chief safeguard for a Christian people against the inroads of heresy, or infidelity.

The essentials, then, negatively expressed, were in the mind of the Church at large, when Prayer Book revision was mentioned, that no changes should be made of such a character that users of the Prayer Book would ever notice that anything had been altered; and that, furthermore, no changes should be made that could in any remotest degree affect doctrinal statements or standards.

It is obvious that when the essentials of Prayer Book revision are thus negatively stated, nothing very hopeful is to be expected in the way of revision. The hope of the present hour rests in the fact that nothing less than a revolution has occurred in the general temper of the Church. The essentials today are expressed not negatively but positively. While it cannot be claimed that sheer conservatism and theological timidity have entirely passed away, it may be said with fairness that they are negligible elements today in the face of proposed revision. Revision is demanded, and it is demanded on two great positive grounds. One of these is a demand for a larger use of the great liturgical treasures of the past. The other is the demand that the Prayer Book should be made the most powerful and efficient instrument possible in meeting the religious needs of the day, whether for worship, or for the guidance and unfolding of the life of individual Christians.

Much good work has been done in the last forty years in liturgical study; and while it is true that liturgical scholars may be few, the suspicion has become very widespread throughout the Church that there are material and traditions, to be derived from the liturgical experience of past ages, which ought to be available for the Prayer Book users of today. On the other hand, the Church has been awakening to the needs of the hour. The religious enthusiasms of her people find expression in missionary and educational endeavor, in ideals for the world-wide extension of the Kingdom, and in various forms of social service; while the satisfaction and cultivation of the spiritual life, along the lines which we may term the "newer mysticism," have been becoming ever more deeply realized. It has been felt that the Prayer Book of the Church is not adequately giving expression to these enthusiasms and satisfactions, and that if the Church is to be a living power and really to do the work which she feels within herself that she may do, that then the Book of Common Prayer must be revised to meet her needs and the needs of the people who look to her. This feeling which was growing in volume before the war, has been vastly increased and hurried forward as a result of war-experiences. The impatience with anything but realities of which we have heard so much, and which is an undoubted sign of the times, has inevitably swept aside those attitudes of sheer conservatism and theological timidity of which I have spoken. If the Church is to be prepared to do her part in the world, and to minister to the people who look to her, there can be no place for conservatism and timidity. She must even be prepared to take great risks in her ventures of faith.

This changed attitude which is an undoubted fact and must be universally recognized by thoughtful Church people gives great hope for a significant and thorough-going revision of the Book of Common Prayer.

It may be interesting to compare the attitude of the Church at the time of the last revision with the Church's attitude today, and it is undoubtedly worth our while to understand the differences as expressed, for instance, in the Resolutions of 1880 and 1913. It is a curious fact, and one which gives us a warning as to the difficulties of reading history by means of Convention Resolutions, that the Resolution of 1880 was in its phraseology much more generous and in appearance more friendly to thorough-going revision than the Resolution of 1913. The Resolution of 1880 in establishing the Joint Commission, asked this Commission to "consider and to report whether, in view of the fact that this Church is soon to enter upon the second century of its organized existence in this country, the changed conditions of the national life do not demand certain alterations in the Book of Common Prayer in the direction of liturgical enrichment and increased flexibility of use." The phraseology of this Resolution, which was due to the large vision of Dr. Huntington, has to be understood, however, in the light of the attitudes and discussions which surrounded it. The atmosphere was full of apprehension and this was so clearly understood by the Commission itself that the Commission's very first act was the adoption of a self-denying ordinance in which they gave expression to those negative essentials of revision which were at that time written into the mind of the Church. They proceeded to express by resolution their conviction that "no alteration should be made touching either statements or standards of doctrine" and that "in all its suggestions and acts, the Commission should be guided by those principles of liturgical construction and ritual use which have made the Book what it is."

The Resolution of 1913 seems very much less generous and large-minded. The Commission is "to consider and report such revision and enrichment as will adapt the Book to present conditions, if in their judgment such revision be necessary." But furthermore, the Resolution of 1913 has embodied in itself two provisos,—one being that "no proposition involving the faith and doctrine of the Church should be considered or reported," and second,—that "no proposal to change the title-page of the Book or the name of the Church should be referred to the Commission." The second of these provisos gives us an explanation of how it happened that the Resolution which inaugurated the present revision was so far from reflecting the temper of the Church. There is no doubt that the temper of the Church was very much more generous towards revision in 1913 than in 1880, and that as has already been stated, the motives of obstructionist conservatism and theological timidity were very much in abeyance, but it had happened that the Church had just been passing through a heated debate as to the change in name, and it was the sensitiveness resulting from this experience that made the Resolution fail in its expression of the Church's temper. When the present Commission met, it was so far from passing any self-denying ordinances that it quickly came to the conclusion not only that revision was desirable, but that everything in the way of revision was open to it for consideration, and that since in a sense every alteration, even to commas and capitalization, involved doctrine, that no considerations of theological timidity should stand in the way of proposals for revision, provided those proposals fairly met liturgical standards and truly served the religious needs of the hour. In this attitude the Commission was undoubtedly reflecting what was truly the temper of the Church. There was no reason why it should not do so, since the Commission was a fair reflection of the Church as a whole. It represented every part of the Church, geographically and theologically. It contained in itself all kinds of churchmen and all points of view. That it was right in its position was amply verified by the way in which the Church accepted the Commission's first report in 1916. Comment from all sides, spoken and written, however critical about details, was practically unanimous in approval of the general attitude as to revision, and the test vote of the Convention in 1916, as to whether the Church wanted revision, and, if so, in general wanted the kind of revision proposed, was a practically unanimous vote in favor of the procedure outlined. A good illustration of the change of temper, so far as theological timidity is concerned, may be given by one concrete example. It was as true in 1880 as in 1913 that those who considered the matter at all, and were sensitive to liturgical demands, felt the need of revision in the opening invocations of the Litany. These invocations are unfortunately repetitious, misleading in their emphasis on the phrase "miserable sinners," inconsistent in their characterizations of the persons of the Trinity through the introduction of the "filioque" in the third invocation, and awkward in phraseology. When one is concerned, as the present Commission has been, with purely liturgical considerations, and with the desire to meet the needs of the worshipping congregation, it was a simple matter to suggest a revision of these invocations. No hesitation was expressed as to recommending such revision; and when the recommendation was set before the Church in 1916, no protests, so far as I am aware, were heard in regard to such recommendation. By contrast, in 1880, because of the predominance of the spirit of theological timidity, and because these invocations must assuredly "touch" or "involve" doctrine, the suggestion for revision was not even for one instant allowed in the Commission, and the proposal for a revision of the Litany in this respect was an impossible proposal to put before the Church.

While recognizing the great gain which has come through the substitution of positive for negative essentials in the matter of revision, we must not, however, be unjust to those principles or attitudes which the assertion of negative essentials do emphasize today, so far as they exist. Let us consider how far there is truth in the demands which they express, and how far these demands ought to be fairly met in the processes of revision.

First, let us consider the significance which attaches to that attitude which I have designated as sheer conservatism. What is really desired is that the worshipping Christian should be undisturbed in the enjoyment and satisfaction which come to him from the use of the Book of Common Prayer. The devout communicant does not wish to feel that when he goes to church he will find himself a stranger there because of a radically altered Prayer Book. He cannot bear to think that the precious heritage of the ages is to be thrown aside and a new Prayer Book substituted in its place. With this sentiment we are probably all in sympathy; and the fact is that the worshipper has nothing to fear from even the most thorough-going revision of the book, for it is not proposed to alter in any essential part the great outlines of the services of the people's worship. The offices of Morning and Evening Prayer, of Litany, and of the Holy Communion, are established, and approve themselves as great instruments of worship. They are by virtue of their own excellence inviolable. No rubrics or precautions are necessary to preserve their integrity. It is possible to enrich them by permissive uses or variations. But nothing is proposed, or likely to be proposed, that will make their beloved forms unrecognizable to the constant and grateful worshipper. It is therefore possible for the most ardent and enthusiastic advocate of thorough-going revision to say to the apprehensive lover of the Prayer Book, that nothing proposed is really going to hurt his sensibilities, or to render the book anything essentially different from what it has been as the instrument of his worship. Furthermore, it is to be remembered that those items which aside from the outlines of the services most strongly commend the book to the lover and user are the Prayer Book version of the Psalter and the body of Collects which the book contains, and it is not contemplated by advocates that either of these parts of the book should be removed or substantially altered. The conservative is really therefore secure in his position. The thorough-goingness of revision will manifest itself most of all in the Occasional Offices; and here I am convinced that the public opinion of the vast body of Church people is more than ready for revision. It is true that there are many people who may not realize this desire until their attention is called to the possibilities of improvement and enrichment. But the occasional participation of the people in these services, from the very fact that it is occasional, renders them less sensitive to change; and the changes which may be incorporated are almost sure to commend themselves, if noticed at all, as helpful alterations.

Passing now to the other negative essential in revision, which in past years has been much in the mind of the Church, what are we to say as to the matter of theological timidity? It seems clear that this attitude, once so prevalent, has been abandoned, because the Church as a whole has very generally come to an understanding of what really has been meant by this instinctive and heretofore unexplained apprehension.

It is not that any one really for a moment imagines that any processes of revision, conducted by a Commission composed of bishops, priests, and laymen, representing all parts of the Church, could for a moment propose anything which would be subversive of the Church's faith,—meaning by the "Church's faith" the Church's ultimate loyalties.   It is, furthermore, inconceivable—(and this is becoming generally understood)— that a Commission which is concerned with liturgical revision, is proposing for a moment to attempt any alteration of statements of doctrine in Creeds or elsewhere.   If the Church ever esteems such revision to be desirable, it will undertake it consciously and deliberately by a special process inaugurated for that purpose; and doubtless in connection with the Christian consciousness of the whole Church, and not through the reaction of any one part of it.   It is probably a pretty generally accepted position in regard to this matter, that even in such details as the possible elimination of the "filioque" in the Nicene Creed, or the possible addition of the fourth note to the notes of the Church in the same Creed, that it would be better for the American Church, when acting in this matter, to act in cooperation with at least the other branches of the Anglican Communion.   The phrases, therefore, to which the Church has given currency through its provisos in the past as to "touching doctrine" can obviously have nothing to do with what may be termed the essentials of the faith.   A further study of the situation makes it clear that it is nothing less than absurd to assume that such provisos are intended as prohibitions against any alterations in forms or prayers where doctrines are embedded or mentioned.   This would effectively put a stop to all liturgical revision,—since there is no question even of a word, a capital, or a comma where doctrine may not ultimately be involved.

But it furthermore becomes clear to the mind of the Church that if by doctrine is meant a belief or pious opinion, which has currency in the Church at some given time, it is not only conceivable but inevitable that it may be desirable and right to "touch doctrine" by making changes.   It is obvious, for instance, today, that a belief in regard to God's relation to sickness, suffering, and death which was at one time prevalent, and which has an altogether disaproportionte expression in the

Book of Common Prayer, is now no longer prevalent, and requires elimination or at least modification, and the avoidance of that disproportionate emphasis which in itself leads to error. There is also apparent readiness on the part of the whole Church, in all its parties or schools of thought, to repudiate the once current belief in original sin, as that doctrine was technically and exactly defined, wherever that doctrine is or appears to be embedded in the Book of Common Prayer, as in connection, for instance, with the Church's thought of Baptism.

Nor is it altogether in relation to what may be esteemed outgrown opinions that the process of liturgical revision seems to demand that doctrine be touched. There is a belief current everywhere today in the rightness of prayers for the departed, which is demanding expression in the people's book of worship, and asking at any rate that this book should allow for the expression of such belief in a prayer.

The situation, then, seems to be this. There is absolutely no cause for apprehension as regards the ultimate loyalties, and there is, on the other hand, an irresistible demand for re-statements so far as certain doctrines and belief are concerned, or at least for marked changes of emphasis in liturgical expression. We are thus driven to ask the question as to what is the real significance of that apprehension which in the past has insisted upon provisos regarding doctrine, and which still insists upon these today. The answer to this question has, through the processes of past and present revision, very clearly emerged, and it is this: nothing in the way of revision must be attempted which shall in any way imperil that fundamental principle which lies at the basis of the book and at the basis of the Church's life, and which we may term the principle of comprehension. It is by virtue of this principle that the Book and Church alike belong equally and completely both to the Catholic-minded and to the Protestant-minded member and worshipper. This was the difficult experiment which the Reformation settlement inaugurated, and which on the whole the history of the last four hundred years has splendidly vindicated. It finds its crowning expression in the Book of Common Prayer in the never to be forgotten fact that in the administration of the Lord's Supper, the Catholic-minded sentence at the time of the distribution of the elements, of the first Book of Edward VI, and the Protestant-minded sentence of the second Book of Edward VI, are said in their entirety, one after the other, in the form of a complete and undivided utterance. What is really demanded by the theological proviso is that nothing shall be done to imperil this great principle. There may be extension, along either line, provided such extension does not imperil in any way the Book's usability to either the Catholic-minded or the Protestant-minded worshipper. To state the matter in a somewhat badly negative fashion, nothing must be done in the way of revision which shall render the book any less completely and truly than it is today the possession alike of Catholic-minded and Protestant-minded men. Nothing must be done which shall make either one less at home in the midst of the worshipping congregation. This is the essential matter in that negative demand which we have termed theological timidity. This is the rightness in that which has sometimes appeared to be unreasoning apprehension. It is moreover my belief that this rightness is universally recognized throughout the whole Church, and that there is no desire anywhere to make capital out of the processes of revision for either of the great elements which together constitute the strength of the Church's life, and give it its significant part in the processes that lead towards Church unity. I can at any rate testify to this: and it is a testimony that I believe ought to be given wide currency, that in the present Commission with which it has been my privilege to work for the last six years, this conviction dominates. If the Commission fairly represents the total Church, as I believe it does, it is a striking testimony to the Church's attitude in this matter. With absolute frankness of expression, with the most clean-cut and uncompromising setting forth of different points of view, there has been throughout the work of the Commission an absolute harmony of spirit, a generous and whole-hearted determination to carry on the processes of revision with a single eye to liturgical effectiveness, and with a gracious and insistent recognition of the principle of comprehension as vital to the Church's integrity of life, in work and worship.

Let us turn now to the consideration of those positive demands which have become today vital essentials in the matter of Prayer Book revision. These are the demands, as has been said, which spring out of what we may call the "liturgical renaissance" and the religious demands of the day.

By "liturgical renaissance" is meant the outstanding fact that throughout Christendom there has come into existence a growing consciousness of the vast liturgical treasures existent in ancient liturgies and forms, the proved excellences of which are available for the Christian worshipper today, and which ought more largely to be drawn upon for the Church's benefit. The fact is, that the study of liturgics, has made great progress in the last generation or two. There are notable liturgical scholars who have made great contributions to our knowledge, and the fact of existent treasures not now in use but available has permeated generally, though perhaps vaguely, through the consciousness of Christian people. This is manifested everywhere, not only in those churches we are sometimes pleased to call historic. A certain group of Christians, for instance, which the Catholic and orthodox person would unhesitatingly designate as a sect, and as an heretical sect, in a recent revision of its forms of worship has made use, in its order for the Lord's Supper, of the outline given in the Didaché. Another body of Christians has incorporated in like manner in its form for the administration of the Lord's Supper the Benedictus qui venit, without apparently any debate as to possible doctrinal implications. It is to be expected, then, that our own Church will be awake to opportunities of a like nature, and that in the revision now in progress, and in forms which may be laid before the Church in the future, there will be increasingly a drawing upon ancient sources, and a larger use of Christendom's accumulations of liturgical material. In the proposals which the present Commission is about to lay before the Church, there will be found indications of this process. They will be felt to be perhaps on the whole slight. They are nevertheless real and helpful, and possibly more significant as to the future than as to the present. They will be discovered in certain permissive enrichments in the order for the Holy Communion; in the significant and helpful new office for the Visitation of the Sick; in a proposed new and short Litany for Ordinations, derived from ancient sources, and in individual instances, in certain prayers, versicles, and responses, and minor forms.

The promise for the future can be as well illustrated as in any other way by the possibility which certainly exists for enrichment, some time in some way, of the whole body of Collect material within the Book of Common Prayer. A study of the present body of Collects of the Christian Year reveals the fact that they are too universally tinged with the Augustinianism of Western Christendom, and that in spite of the amazing excellence of so many of the Latin Collects, there is, nevertheless, a striking poverty of ideas, burdensome amount of repetition, and a decided over-emphasis, as might be expected from the sources, upon the judicial conception theology in, and upon the constantly recurring ideas of punishment and reward. The book of worship, which is to be the abidingly satisfying instrument for the prople's devotions, ought to find place for expression in prayer of joy in the thought of God and his creation, of the sense of relationship as the basis and incentive of human desire and aspiration, of adoration, in the Presence, of affirmation as well as petition in the apprehension of God's being and beauty. Such expressions may be found in the Oriental rites, and will doubtless in time be appropriated and adapted.

The other positive essential realized by us today is based, as has been said, upon the religious demands of the time. If we look into the heart of our life today and ask ourselves what are the bases of the religious aspirations and enthusiasm of our people, we shall find them to rest on such ideals as are expressed by the terms "the extension of Christ's kingdom," "the federation of the world," "Christian service," "social justice;"to show themselves in varying manifestations of quietism or mysticism, finding expression in classes in personal religion, and in other groups of worshipping Christians, whose hearts are set upon the ulimate realities. It needs no argument to show that the Book of Common Prayer as it exists today is peculiarly lacking in providing adequate expression for these needs and enthusiasms. This ought not so to be. The demand of the day is that the Book should at least make a beginning of providing prayers and suggesting opportunities for the expression in worship of people whose hearts are set upon the great Christian enterprises of today and, who cannot be led on in their devotions and consecrations by slavish adherence to forms which give no expression to such desires. To give a concrete illustration of the demand which is made as a result of this essential in revision, it ought to happen that in the Book as revised there shall be found prayers for Christian Service and for Social Justice. This is so true that the Church will probably come to the conclusion that it is more important to have such prayers, than to wait for an entirely satisfying expression in prayers or Forms of Service. It is not easy to find or make a truly satisfactory expression for these needs, but the vitally important thing is to have an expression; it will be better for the Church to accept as a part of its Book a prayer which confessedly does not altogether worthily compare with the Book's great prayer utterances than to refuse to have any prayer at all. Of course, the inclusion of prayers in the Prayers and Thanksgivings to touch these vital needs and to supply with reality the Church's prayer utterances of today is far from meeting the requirements of the situation. These may, however, be met in revision in another manner.

This manner is the frank adoption on the part of the Church of a principle of liberty and flexibility. This can be attained in the first place by adopting a general rubric which in essence will magnify the responsibility of the priest as the leader of the people's worship, and will give him the priveleges and opportunity of using forms of worship of many kinds and sorts as the need may seem to demand. The great offices of the Church stand, and stand in their integrity, as the finest and most effective expressions for public worship. There is no fear of their losing their power and persistence. The power and persistence reside in themselves and in their greatness. On times and occasions, however, they will be put aside for an entirely different form of expression. This form may be modern or it may on the other hand be derived from ancient sources. It will be real; it will give expression to what is needing expression at the moment. It will be the inspiration for the assembled people, whose gathering together may be in the interest of missions or of social service or of religious education, or may be, on the other hand, for the realization of God's presence through the fellowship in silence, and in the great affirmations of faith. The priest must be free to arrange and order the worship as required, but it is also true that he will often desire the help of wise suggestion for the ordering of the service and for the leadership of the people. It is therefore quite possible that it may be desirable that offices and forms should be suggested and available and that in order that they may be readily in the hands of the people, that these offices and forms should be bound up with the Book of Common Prayer as a sort of appendix to that Book. It would be premature to recommend perhaps in most instances, insertion in the Book of Common Prayer, to take their place beside the great offices. There are none of these forms today that do not need the process of testing. They ought to have the opportunity of this testing; and this may be accomplished if they are generally available for the use of congregations. The time may then come when one or another of them will win its place within the book itself.

It becomes indeed more and more obvious that, in a general way, the method by which we are to meet the demands of the hour is primarily through frank recognition of the fact of the responsibility which must be thrown upon the priest as the leader of the people's worship. In the matter, for instance, of the lections, it ought ot be frankly recognized, whatever the phraseology of the rubric, that the fundamental principle as to the selection of lessons in Morning and Evening Prayer, is that it rests with the priest to select the lessons. Where the need of the moment is clear and obvious, that selection must be a free and original selection. On the other hand, as the year unfolds itself, the priest will desire the helpfulness which comes from suggestions offered by tables of lessons. These should be understood to be suggestions. They should be excellent suggestions, and should be comprehensive, and intelligently ordered, and with variety of choices. The same principle obtains in regard to the Psalms, a principle which was accepted by the last Convention. The basis is the priest's selection, a selection guided, however, by the best tables of selection which can be provided. This principle may be in measure extended even to those lections which are embodied in the Communion office. The Epistles and Gospels stand, as a rule, fixed and printed upon the page. But it is a suggestion which will probably commend itself to the Church that in the case of week day Communion the priest may select at his discretion, for the Epistle and Gospel, passages from the Scripture lessons of the given week.

This same responsibility of the priest as leader of the people's worship is leading us to a realization of the proper understanding of a rubric. It was a wise bishop of the English Church who said not many years ago, "I long to see a plain recognition of the fact that a rubric records simply how things are done (unless there is valid reasons for other course) and that it is not a Canon, the function of which is to prescribe how things shall be done." This utterance, which was of the nature of a prophecy, is rapidly winning fulfillment. We have great opportunity in the American Church to realize very clearly what is the nature of the true rubric. True, that is, not only in its present usefulness, but in its historic origin. We are beginning to understand that it is not a law which requires obedience, but a helpful suggestion or direction to be followed where applicable. Nothing in the history of the English Church, or of our Church, should lead us away from a fuller apprehension of this principle. The English Church is, of course, hampered in rediscovering the true rubric by the existence of the laws of conformity, in virtue of which rubrics became acts of Parliament. We are free from this disability. It is true we have embedded in our Book fragments of ancient canon law under the guise of rubric. But since they are under the guise of rubrics, they become happily ineffective as law, and amendable to the true rubrical definition, and so in general innocuous. Of course it may be said that this understanding of the nature of a true rubric, and its advocacy as a principle, has its dangers. It probably has. But we can afford to risk the perils. In fact we must do so, if we are to be a living Church and to meet the demands of reality. The safeguard is, of course, in a well-trained ministry; and the dangers are after all negligible as compared with the dangers which result from the strict-constructionist attitude.

The essential, then, in Prayer Book revision which resides in the religious demands of the day is to be met in a two-fold way. First, by a frank recognition of the *jus liturgicum* of the priest, and of his freedom and responsibility as leader of the people's worship. And second, by assisting him towards intelligent and helpful leadership by an ever-increasing body of suggestions, through rubrics offering in many cases alternate suggestions, through wisely ordered tables for guidance in choosing his lections, and through actual suggested forms for offices which shall provide the worshipping people with the required elements of freshness and modernity and reality. We are likely to go farther in these directions in the future than the present Commission will recommend. In the matter, for instance, of the order for the Holy Communion which is, in the nature of the case, a subject which leads to debate and to the most careful consideration, it may very well happen that the time will come when through some rubrical provision there will be opportunity given for the use of a shorter form of this office. There are some today who realize keenly this need. There are times when the effectiveness of worship might very well be enhanced by making it more distinctly eucharistic, leaving its large elements of preparation, through examination and confession and instruction, to be provided for at some previous service of preparation. Agitation in England with regard to this matter is significant. A large body of priests of the English Church desire the privilege of using instead of the English office, the office in the first Book of Edward VI or the Scottish office, or the American office. Liberal churchmen in England are favoring this permissive alternate use, and frankly on the ground that it might in time lead to still another alternate, an alternate which instead of emphasizing, in the use of the office either the thought of sacrifice, or the thought of the satisfying of the individual soul, should emphasize "the kingdom," and be so framed as to be the culminating expression in worship of the aspirations of those who labor for World Justice and World Peace: an ideal which is not without historical vindication in some of the most ancient outlines of the office.

It will be recognized that the two essentials which have been outlined as the positive essentials which form the dominating demands to-day in the matter of Prayer Book revision, if held together as they must inevitably be, will tend, as they are realized, to establish and strengthen that underlying principle of comprehension of which I have already spoken. The demand which rests in the "liturgical renaissance," by the very nature of the case, leads to the satisfying of the Catholic-minded, while the demand which rests upon the religious requirements of the day, in the same way by the very nature of the case, tends to meet the needs of the Protestant-minded.

We may thus rest satisfied and unapprehensive in the phenomena of the present day as they exhibit themselves in the whole process of Prayer Book Revision—believing that nothing will be lost which ought to be preserved, and that if the Church is fearless and faithful, she will gain much that she needs to gain in her ability to meet not only the needs of her own adherents, and especially the needs of her worshipping congregations, but the needs of the total Christianity of our land. The great incentive which lay behind the modern processes of Prayer Book revision, as inaugurated by Dr. Huntington in 1880, was the incentive for Christian unity. This same incentive is, in the last analysis, today the primary demand and the final assumption in the revision of the Book of Common Prayer.

ESSENTIALS OF PRAYER BOOK REVISION

By Howard Baldwin St. George

THE Title of this topic may lead to some misconception. It may be taken by some to mean that the formularies of Worship, and for the Administration of the Sacraments and other Rites of the Church, as at present set forth in the Book of Common Prayer, are not sufficient to inculcate, explicitly or implicitly, the whole of the Catholic faith and practice, and that therefore essential revision includes provision for the recognition of certain aspects of belief and practice hitherto disallowed in the American Church. To such a position I would unhesitatingly demur. In my judgment the Commission is not making any proposal for revision of any formularies, or adding to any Rite, or instituting any practice which is not at least implicitly sanctioned by the Book of Common Prayer as it stands. The possible exceptions to this statement might be (1) the provision for the administration of Holy Communion in Church by the method of Intinction, (2) the provision for the administration of the Holy Communion to the sick by the method of the Reserved Sacrament, (3) the insertion in the order for the Visitation of the Sick of the form for Anointing with oil in the Name of the Lord, and (4) the addition of the Rite for the Admission to the Office of Deaconess. The last will perhaps be the most difficult to justify on the ground of Catholic tradition and practice, but the attempt will be made to show that even in this respect it has a claim to recognition agmonst the proposals for revision, even as the others mentioned. These, with others, are in the nature of recovery or restoration, of practices which had fallen into abeyance, or which for some reason, at the time considered compelling, had been discontinued but which the condition and needs of the Church today demand. They are not essential but important and highly desirable.

If then I am asked what *are* the essentials in Prayer Book Revision, I do not name this or that particular proposal but I mean the recognition of certain Liturgical principles which from the 16th century have been greatly obscured, it not completely forgotten.

A new method of Liturgical revision and compilation was adopted at the time of the Reformation. This was equally the case at Rome and Canterbury. One man, or a small group of men, in each instance dominated the situation. The Council of Trent placed the work in the hands of the Pope; the Council of Regency in England entrusted the work to the Archbishop of Canterbury. In both cases a small Commission seems to have been appointed. In neither case do we learn anything about the details of the work. Only the result is shown. In neither case was the judgment of the Church asked. The Roman Missal was imposed by the Bull of Pious V, 1570. The Book of Common Prayer was imposed by the Act of Uniformity, 1549. In both cases the rule for the use of the revised liturgies was absolute and iron clad. "Mass shall be sung or said according to the rite, manner, and standard which is given in this Missal; nor in celebrating Mass shall anyone dare to add or recite other ceremonies or prayers than those that are contained therein." (Bull *Quo primum* of Pious V, 1570.) By the Act of Uniformity, 1549, and subsequent Acts precisely the same attitude was taken with regard to the Book of Common Prayer. "All ministers be bounden to say and use the Matins, Evensong, Celebration of the Lord's Supper commonly called the Mass, and the administration of each of the Sacraments, . . . in such Order and Form as is mentioned in the same Book and none other or otherwise." (2 and 3 Ed. VI, cap. I.)

In addition then to the new method of revision, there was introduced the new principle of liturgical uniformity. Not only is the voice and consent of the Church ignored but also the traditional *jus liturgicum* of the episcopate is set aside. It may be urged with much cogency that the conditions of the times, the fierce theological controversies that were raging, the ecclesiastical anarchy which prevailed necessitated these innovations in liturgical procedure. But it has become impressed on the Anglican Communion, until it is almost an obsession, that the arrangement arrived at between 1552 and 1662, what is loosely and commonly designated as "the Reformation Settlement," is the final word in matters of theological opinion and liturgical expression for the Church of England and those Churches in communion with her. Now this rigidity of use is not only at variance with the natural and historical development of liturgical formularies, but also carries many evils in its train.

(a) Every student of the subject knows that from the beginning, both in the East and the West, Rites and formularies developed quite freely, and that in the first instance entirely apart from Synodical or even episcopal authority. The mention of the number and diversities of Liturgies is sufficient to establish this point. It belonged to the Bishop, or the group of Bishops in Synod, to endorse, or regulate or direct the use of this or that liturgical formulary, or devotional use in Rite and Ceremony. In numbers of instances accretions crept in in the Mass and Office, in Anthem and prayer, exhibiting development in enrichment both in the Rite as a whole and in particular parts, which became accepted without any official sanction as far as history shows. As an illustration contrast the Roman Liturgy in the time of Gregory the Great with the Sarum development in the later middle Ages, and one can readily perceive the tremendous difference between the plain severity of the former and the exuberant diversity and richness of the latter. Now the point is that all this addition of liturgical formularies, development and enrichment in worshipful expression and devotional aspiration, was not the result of revision by authority, was not imposed from above as a determined and fixed feature, but beginning in one Church or diocese, was copied by another and so imperceptibly passed from one place to another until it had become the common use or practice of a province or nation, perhaps of the whole Western Church. In a word it was through the liturgies and in the rites and ceremonies of the Church that the piety and devotion of the faithful were expressed. The rigidity and uniformity has been to divert this desire for the opportunity of devotional expression into other channels. It is in this way that the great variety and number of what are termed "popular devotions," e. g., of the Sacred Heart, have sprung up and developed in the Roman Communion.

What has been the effect of rigid uniformity in the Anglican Communion? Practically it has gone by the board, though there are to be found those who still cling to it as an ideal. But how has it worked in the past? From the first it was imposed under severe penalty, and, because the attempt was made to silence popular devotion, schism rent the Church of England. The Independents left England because there they could worship in *one way* and *one way only* and so today we are confronted with American Congregationalism. Wesley and his high church friends could not invade the college chapel for prayer meeting and the other pious methods desired in the expression of their spiritual life, and later when the movement inaugurated by him spread and gained impetus, the people whom he had converted and taught to pray and sing hymns were denied the use of the parish churches because the devotions were not in accordance with the Book of Common Prayer as by law established.

Now with our inheritance of a standardized Prayer Book imposed by the authority of the General Convention is there any escape from the rigidity which has hitherto bound us? And is it possible in any real way to take into account and give recognition to services and devotions which seem to be called out by special needs or special conditions, or have gained for themselves a certain amount of use and popularity? That there are such services, we are all well aware. For example, there is that very popular one used so generally on Good Friday, known as the "Three Hours Service," which calls forth no remark, even if it is borrowed from the Roman Communion. But it has no legal status, perhaps in some instances it is licenced by individual Bishops, on the power given in the general rubric,

"Concerning the services of the Church." It is *essential* then that the scope of this general rubric should be widened so as to facilitate the use of extra-liturgical services, always subject to the regulation of the Bishop. It does not seem to be necessary that in every instance the Bishop's licence should be first obtained, though that may be desirable to promote confidence, but it means that the service, or devotions, or formularies, whatever they may be, both as to arrangement and matter should be put to the test of use, as to whether they really meet the religious aspirations and devotional needs of the people.

It may be said that the method provided under the Constitution and Canons of the Church is sufficient to secure the necessary popular recognition, but experience has shown that such is not always the case. This applies especially to new services, new prayers, new versicles and responses. General Convention, for the most part, meets such proposals seriously for the first time when they come before the Convention. Then a snap judgment is passed upon them and they are amended or otherwise dealt with by a vote. Consider the nature of prayer, the aspiration of the soul towards God, the expression of the soul's desires and needs, and then think of it as being bandied about from one side of the Convention to another and finally allowed to come to rest a "pieced and patched" affair, and the prayer is adopted as often as not through impatience at delay or from weariness of spirit. Not thus are the best results secured. Liturgical formularies are searched out or thought out by those to whom the subject is congenial, in the quiet of sympathetic surroundings. Anyone who has tried knows the difficulty of finding the right phraseology in which to express the subject of the prayer and the proper form in which it should be cast, so as to conform to the traditional rules of liturgical propriety. But the mere reading over of a prayer, once or more, often does not indicate what its value will be when incorporated into public worship. The question is, will it stand the test of use? The same test ought to be applied to all new matter proposed for adoption. But the procedure by which we are bound, precludes the possibility of any such experimental use. It is true that the matter lies before the Church for three years, that every diocese receives official notification that it has been adopted, and it is possible that the proposed changes are subjected to the more or less careful scrutiny of a committee appointed for that purpose, but that does not furnish the necessary experience. It seems to me to be *essential* in the matter of Prayer Book Revision, that some provision should be made whereby the charges adopted at one General Convention should be allowed a tentative use for six years or at the least, three years. In the interim a small Committee of the Commission, say seven in number, should meet from time to time to receive and examine criticisms based upon actual use in the services of the Church.

It would be the business of the Committee as far as possible to obtain detailed information as to how far the changes thus permitted had been brought into use, how far they seemed to meet the needs of the Church's devotional life or the special purpose for which they were put forth and what amendments seemed desirable. The Committee would then be in a position to collect, tabulate and weigh the available evidence in favor of amendment, ratification or discontinuance. This evidence should be reviewed by the whole Commission and its conclusions as now, issued as its report. The General Convention thus would have in definite form the result of what would be in the nature of a referendum to the people. The vote should be taken on each several offices without debate, either to accept or reject, or postpone for three years. "To postpone" would permit the continued use of the changes recommended by the Commission, and thus give further time in which to determine their value.

It does not seem that such a procedure would present any great difficulty. As a matter of fact the Commission proposes an Appendix to the Prayer Book, comprising with a number of new prayers, some offices, such as a Litany, Compline, a solemn Thanksgiving, in order that their value may be tested by use and experience. What is to hinder a joint resolution of General Convention to the effect that "such proposals for revision of

offices and formularies and all additions in the nature of enrichment which have been adopted in one General Convention,
shall be printed as an Appendix to the Prayer Book, and their
use be allowed until next General Convention." Then provision could be made for the appointment of the Committee,
with powers, as already indicated. Such in barest outline is the
suggestion for a scheme, which seems practicable, and which
would go a long way towards making effective what I consider to be essential principles of liturgical revision, viz., the
recognition of the fact (1) that forms of worship and devotion have never remained stationary but are largely the outcome of the spiritual outlook and devotional temperament of
peoples, influenced by the needs of time and circumstances in
which they live, and therefore (2) that provision ought to be
made for diversity in liturgical worship under legitimate but
liberal regulation. The Commission has tried to meet the first
and the second by recommending a large discretion in the use
of permissive formularies, by proposals to incorporate into the
services many features which have already obtained the sanction of custom. The attempt in the interest of traditional
uniformity to insist on a form of worship which has no particular
appeal to (a) people, drawn to us from all nations and tongues,
and with every kind of religious inheritance, is to kill devotion
and empty Churches. Morning Prayer for instance may be
satisfactory as the chief service of the Lord's Day in the settled
and conservative parishes in the East and the South. With
them it is no doubt a matter of traditional inheritance, and an
intelligent appreciation of its helpfulness as an act of worship.
But in the younger part of the country where "what happened
in England at the Reformation" excites no interest, the newer
Americans and converts to other communions are repelled by
the complexity and difficulty and wearisomeness of this office.
The exhortation is an anachronism and its language archaic;
Cranmer's great Reformation principle in regard to the regular
recitation of the Psalter is no longer possible to maintain with
edification in the average church, the lessons are too long, and,
as a rule, that from the old Testament unedifying to the aver-

age congregation; criticism is voiced of the length of the *Te Deum*, especially when it is made the subject of elaborate musical rendition; the *Benedicite* is not only long but monotonous and its meaning not very obvious if not to the ordinary church goer at any rate to those trying to become familiar with the Church's worship. Little is left of the original structure of the Office to call out the spirit of worshipful devotion, or to help to edification. If then Morning Prayer is to hold its place as an integral part of the Church's system of worship—and the fact is recognized that there are people to whom its appeal is paramount—still it is essential that such revision shall be effected which will render the service more adaptable to the present day needs of the people. The Commission in its recommendations attempts to do this. It safeguards the tradition, but allows for flexibility in use, especially in the Psalter. Compression is suggested when the Holy Communion is to follow. Whether the result will meet the expectations is a mooted point. The impression seems to be gaining ground that except in the influential churches of our large cities Morning Prayer not only no longer attracts, but as a matter of fact is losing its hold on the people. Is it because it lacks definite objective? Perhaps because it never was, in its inception, in its development, or in its use, a "people's Service." It, like clerical celibacy, as Duchesne points out in *Christian Worship*, is a legacy from the monks. Cranmer endeavoured to make it over for popular use, and it must be admitted with considerable success, but it required German mercenaries to quell the initial opposition. That does not sound good to American churchmen in the year following the war!

It was in and through the Divine Liturgy that the people normally expressed themselves in worship and devotion. The Eucharist was from the beginning and everywhere throughout Christendom, the people's service. It is to the people in their response to the Deacon's announcement of the subject of prayer, that we are indebted for the "Lord have mercy!" It was the people who insisted on the particular intercessions in connection with their offering of the Eucharistic Elements so that when we read of "The Prayers of the people" in connection with the liturgy we know exactly what is meant. Our prayer 'for the whole state of Christ's Church' represents this feature. It was the people who insisted on the prayers for the departed being incorporated in the Roman Canon. It was the people who introduced the acclaim, 'Blessed is He that cometh in the Name of the Lord,' as a liturgical formulary. It is fairly safe to say that all outside the official prayers of the celebrant and the lessons, have been the outcome of, or at least greatly influenced by, popular devotion. And the reason is not far to seek. The Eucharist is essentially an objective service. I do not stop to argue the point. I simply assert the fact. There is something objective to be done. There is an objective climax to be reached. That objective is reached by an offering which belongs to the people and with which they are identified. Therefore from its very nature it calls out and it brings them into closest touch with Jesus of Bethlehem, of Calvary, of Olivet, to make intercession, worship, and devotion. It is doing something worth while, for God, before His Divine Majesty. "Wherefore, O Lord and Heavenly Father, we thy humble servants do celebrate and make here before thy Divine Majesty with these thy holy gifts which we now offer unto thee the Memorial thy Son hath commanded us to make." Therefore it is essential that everything that will encourage congregational devotion and worship should be permitted. If the Decalogue seems out of place and discouraging as the opening of the essentially Christian service (see Bishop Gore's paper in "Dominant Ideas") let it be omitted and let us fall back on the simple "Lord have mercy" for our approach. If the singing of a psalm or hymn between the Scripture lessons (as in Morning Prayer) seems fitting and helpful let it be done. Let the familiar "The Lord be with you" recall the people's attention to renewed devotion at each change of direction in the service. If custom has added the "Blessed be he that cometh" to the Sanctus, let it be sanctioned for its devotional value. Above all let the Lord's Prayer become the fitting climax of the Eucharistic Prayer, not simply and solely because it is found so placed in practically every historic liturgy East and West, but because it calls out the devotional coöperation of the people at this point of the service as no other liturgical formulary could, because it shows the Eucharist to be not merely the act of the celebrant, but the corporate prayer of the faithful assembled, and their participation in the holy priesthood of the Christian people.

Not one of these points enumerated is essential to the sufficiency of the Liturgy, but all of them seem essential to enhance its devotional attractiveness, by encouraging the people to take a larger share in its use, and to realize that it is peculiarly their own.

There are four recommendations in the Commission's Report, which may possibly be considered as definite innovations. To enumerate them and indicate their present purpose will justify the action of the Commission as guided by sound liturgical principles.

1. The Office for the Admission of a Deaconess. The position and work of a Deaconess in the early Church is somewhat obscure. However this ministry of women lasted until about the fifth century. Thenceforth the service of women was absorbed in the religious communities. With the suppression of the monasteries the official service of women in the Church of England came to an end until recent times. Now both Deaconesses and Sisters are recognized by the Canons of the American Church. There seems to be a demand for the recognition of the service of women (Deaconesses) in the Rites of the Church. No formulary for the Ordination of a Deaconess appears in the early documents. Having no precedent for a guide the office recommended by the Commission is frankly new. It is based on various Diocesan uses. The Commission has done some editing and recommends that henceforth there shall be but one use.

2. The method of Intinction in the Administration of the Holy Communion in Church. This appears to be subversive of our Lord's command at the Institution at the Last Supper. It also sets aside one of the fundamental principles of the Re-

formation, and the very first liturgical reform inaugurated in England. Yet we are confronted with the fact that an increasing number of communicants decline to receive from the Chalice, for hygienic reasons, and therefore abstain from Communion. Lagarde (the Latin Ch: in Mae) asserts that for much the same reasons as today Intinction was used in the early Middle Ages, but was soon abandoned for Communion in one kind. As no method is indicated in the proposed rubric, and no practical and satisfactory method has yet appeared, it may be that Communion in one kind will be the solution of the difficulty. The Church has acted on the right of regulating the method of administering the Sacraments and accommodating itself to times and circumstances, e. g., substituting 'pouring' for 'immersion' in Baptism. Such may be the case now.

3. The method of Reservation in the Administration of the Holy Communion to the Sick. This has an early and continuous history in the practice of the Church, from A. D. 150 at any rate. It was continued under I. Ed. VI and recognized in the Latin version of the Elizabethan P. B. It is provided for in the Scottish Liturgy. Present day needs under modern conditions of living make Reservation a practical necessity to insure the Communion of the sick at any time under any circumstances. The purpose of the proposed rubric is to place the regulation of the Reservation under the direction of the bishop.

4. The Anointing with Oil, and laying hands on the sick that they may recover. This Ministry to the sick has Scriptural authority and has fairly continuous history from the third century. As a help and comfort both in body and soul to the sick it is much desired and widely used. Many different forms in its administration appear in the liturgical books. In some cases the emphasis has been laid on the recovery of health, in others on spiritual graces. With the form recommended by the Commission, provision is made for either anointing with oil or laying on of hands, where this ministry shall be faithfully desired, the accompanying prayers asking for relief both of body and soul of the sick person.

The fact that not one of these four ministrations is specifically mentioned in the Prayer Book, or that any one of them disappeared at any particular time or for any particular reason, does not militate against the desirability of their recovery and recognition and regulation under the present revision. All to a greater of lesser extent are in use at the present time throughout the Church and have received episcopal endorsement in various processes. The admission of Deaconesses will not cease even if the proposed Office is not adopted. Intinction will probably go on being used even if General Convention withhold its sanction. The same will be true of the use of Reservation and Anointing.

Time forbids to do more than say how necessary and valuable are the recommendations for the Revision for the Offices of Baptism, Confirmation, and the Burial of the Dead. One office for Baptism is made to serve for all occasions. Some unfortunate archaic phraseology and ideas are eliminated, the whole office is simplified and made plain and direct, and above all the sponsorial system is placed on a practical and intelligent basis. Much the same is true of the Order for Confirmation wherein the vows as at Baptism, are made specific and individual and the sense of reality is deepened in the candidate at a very solemn moment in life. The Confirmation form is made analogous to that in Baptism, so that it may be specifically understood what the nature of the Rite is, thus conforming to the use in every rite in the Prayer Book, where the minister, be he bishop or priest, states plainly what is being done.

Of the enrichment of the Order for the Burial of the Dead and the insertion of a definite prayer for the departed it is not necessary to speak, as this was passed by both Houses of the last Convention, but through some technical mistake failed to receive final concurrence.

To return to the topic under discussion. Nothing is essential. Practically all recommended by the Commission, in my judgment, is important and highly desirable. The revision is intended to meet the diversified needs of the Church at this time of immense opportunity and tremendous responsibility.

Timorous souls will dread disaster in one direction or the other; but it will be to the discredit of the American Church if she allows herself to be hampered by petty prejudices and differences in the progressive and Catholic movement to make the Prayer Book of real and practical value to the religious needs of the American people.

PART V

THE NEED OF AN AMERICAN LABOUR PARTY

THE NEED OF AN AMERICAN LABOUR PARTY

By Percy Stickney Grant

A MEETING under the auspices of the Episcopal Church to discuss the problems of labour on May Day (the working-classes' international holiday) is the most timely incident in my experience of the Church. I hope this coincidence (for I am afraid it is nothing more) may be prophetic of a new and closer attention by the Church—which boasts itself the wealthiest in New York—to the outcries of the worker.

The need of a labour party in America is loudly declared by the immediate situation. On the one hand we see the imprisonment of labour leaders which has excited the wrath of the world of labour. On the other hand we have the alleged discovery of bombs in the mail, supposed to be addressed to the enemies of labour. This is a picture of arbitrary force met by senseless violence.

Do we wish such a method of meeting labour problems in America?—one that means hatred between the classes; a government of extra-judicial force and working class of retaliation and terror. This was the Russian method. If we did accept this method could conservatism expect to win? America cannot have a more subservient police or an army more obedient to the dictates of government than those of old Russia, or a people more impotent than the illiterate peasants who were the subjects of the Czar. But in spite of absolutism of privilege and the weakness of the poor, the whole structure of czarism fell to the ground. After such a lesson America can hardly wish to travel in that direction.

Another method of dealing with our labour problem is offered by the British Labour Party. Here is a body made up of groups of students of the labour question—theoretical and practical, organic and political—for the purpose of accomplishing objects which they regard as essential to the welfare of the British working classes. In behalf of the English method this at least can be said—in the past the English by consultation and conciliation—that is by peaceful means—have preserved more of what was substantial, and made steadier gains in political freedom than can be found in any country in Europe.

Not only the advantages of a peaceful method as seen in England, but the affiliation between the American and the English constitution would suggest our looking to England rather than to old Russia for a way of dealing with our labour problem.

But why, it may be asked, do we need to turn to any country, either the country of violence or the country of discussion, to show us the best immediate way? Why will not our present political machinery—at any rate so far as parties go—solve our problems?

Why are not the Republicans and Democrats able to help us out? We must remember that a political party is an instrument of government and that government is that exercise of power by which the state carries out its purposes. The state is an organized population impelled to unity of action by the advantage thus secured in its self-defence and in other efforts to benefit itself. The objects of a state are the promotion of its people's satisfaction in peace and war. A political party being an instrument of government, which is the operating department of a state, wields therefore the state's power or greatly influences it.

I stop here for a moment to call attention to the interesting fact that the clergy have largely supported the theory of the state, which by defining it in terms of contract have rendered it more easily modified and changed than has been encouraged by the theory of divine origin and divine right. For the clergy to consult with sympathy as to ways in which changes and improvements can be brought about in the state, is symptomatic of their past attitude; nor is such an outlook to be wondered at when it is considered that clergymen represent a theory of life which asks and expects vast personal and social transformations, and the widest spread of human advantage.

But let me return to the question why existing parties in America cannot solve the economic problems confronting our government. The one reason is that they do not represent the whole of American life. On the contrary in the exercise of political power, if not in the votes cast at election, they represent a small fraction of the population. A startling illustration of my statement is to be found in recent figures.

CLASS RULE

"The major part of the American population is composed of farmers and wage workers and their families. Of about 40,000,000 persons gainfully employed in the United States, according to the last census, about a third were farmers and farm workers. Of the remainder all except a few hundred thousand were wage workers in industries. There were only a little over 100,000 lawyers in the whole country, or one-quarter of 1 per cent. of the persons engaged in gainful occupations.

"Figures recently have been published by the National Voters' League showing the normal occupations of the personnel of the last Congress. Of the 435 members of the House of Representatives, the great bulk of our farming and labouring population was represented by six farmers and four representatives of labour. Among the 98 members of the Senate were three farmers and no representatives of labour. But in the House sat 306 lawyers and in the Senate 76 more.

"Farmers and farm workers were represented in Congress on the basis of one representative for every one and a third million of such persons. Workingmen in industries were represented on the basis of about one representative for every 5,000,000 or more. But the lawyers were represented on the basis of one for every 400.

"Here is the makeup of the House: Lawyers, 306; business men, 90; newspaper men, 26; farmers, 6; labourers, 4; salesmen and clerks, 5; preachers, 2; educators, 3; physicians, 2; social worker, 1.

"The personnel of the Senate is as follows: Lawyers, 76; business men, 13; newspaper publishers, 2; farmers, 3; physicians, 2.

"In other words, over 90 per cent. of our national legislative body was composed of lawyers, mostly representatives of big interests, and of business men. It would be highly interesting to see a list of the clients of these lawyer-legislators. It, doubtless, would be highly illuminating as to the practical workings of our representative system.

"We commend the above statistics to those scrupulous souls who are wont to decry the new democracies being established throughout eastern and central Europe on the ground that they are class governments. In our Congress one class representing one-fourth of 1 per cent. of the occupational population has upward of 70 per cent. of the representation. The two classes forming upward of 95 per cent. of the occupational population have less than 2½ per cent. of the representation. This is class rule with a vengeance. It explains the bitter resentment of the owning class of this country against any criticism of the old method of purely geographical representation." (*New York Call*, April 27, 1919.)

The second reason for believing existing political parties cannot meet the situation is to be found in their alignment. The Republican Party in recent compaigns has been the party of big business. The Democrat Party the party of small business. Neither one nor the other even attempted to represent labour which was supposed to receive its advantage only from the financial success of big business or small business.

In short, the working people have no political independence. This dependence of the working classes is shown in the difficulty they have with any attempts of legislation in their behalf,— such as a reduction of the hours of labour by state legislation, and the attitude of the courts toward strikes, propaganda, etc.

"President Frank J. Hayes, of the United Mine Workers of America, at the biennial convention of his organization at Indianapolis, in January, 1918, referred to the action of the United States Supreme Court sustaining the injunction which prohibits his organization from soliciting employes of a coal company to become members of the organization, and said:

'In this crisis the Sherman anti-trust act, and other Federal statutes are set aside to permit the formation of exporting trusts and similar pools, some as if by administrative action and some by express congressional laws. It seems, however, to be declared an open season by the Federal judiciary for hunting labour unions; and this convention should not adjourn without taking some decisive steps for laying before Congress the situation raised by these decisions and of securing legislative assurance against their repetition.'"

The last constitutional convention in New York refused the suggestions of the labour unions while the newspapers laughed at their futile attempts to make themselves felt in constitutional revision.

The last Wilson campaign showed clearly the tendency of wealth, in spite of previous party affiliations, to take a determined stand against the increasing power of Mr. Wilson's ideas and influences. In the course of the President's second term his own party has refused his authority. If Mr. Wilson represents the most enlightened statesmanship in America, that is sympathetic with labour's problem, he cannot pledge even the Democrats to his programme.

Again, if labor, judging from the past, can expect nothing from the Republican north it can expect still less from the Democratic south. The traditions of labour there are confused with the prejudices aroused by slavery which associated labour with the negro or with the poor white.

Indeed, in my opinion the unsatisfactory administration of the Department of Justice by Mr. Gregory, and the breakdown of the Post Office Department, wires, and cables, under Mr. Burleson, is nothing more than should have been expected from southerners of their traditions, unsympathetic with the ideals of labour.

If there are reasons for expecting nothing to be done for labour by the Republican and the Democratic Parties, is the same true of the Socialist Party? Is not its ambition to correct false political balances of population to parties here in America? Independently of one's attitude toward the teachings of Socialism, it can be said that Socialism has made rather slow progress in America. It is treated in a doctrinaire method, uncongenial to American political habits, and mostly at the hands of persons from those parts of Europe which have contributed least to our institutions and ideas. If I were a Socialist I would not wait for the triumph of the Socialist Party for influence in the solution of our labour problem.

A further reason for such an attitude toward the Socialist Party is that to help America in the present exigency there must be a much larger organization than the Socialist Party to act as a buffer, and to receive the shock of European proletariat ideas when they strike the United States. We are in the most exposed position of any nation. We are over-represented on the side of property and conservatism, in legislation and in the judiciary, while at the same time labor is relegated to the sidewalk to fight out its vital problems in a turmoil of strikes, with pickets, gunmen, policemen, and tired and confused courts.

There should be a large workingman's party in America which officially could take up, as a matter of national political defence, the economic questions bound to arise. Such a party could employ discussion and publicity to winnow new ideas and to assign the preserved items to political programmes, platforms, etc. Through such striving the workingman could definitely exert his mental and physical energies along constitutional lines at any rate, more carefully, than would be possible in a suddenly provoked, undiscussed or misunderstood revolutionary uprising.

The slow and constitutional methods of a labour party in securing its programme would produce a popular education not only of the proletariat but of the employers, which would be the happiest augury of the stability of the laws finally enacted.

But after all what does labour want? The demands of the British Labour Party may be considered by and large as representing the prospective demands of an American labour party. As expressed in the constitution of the British Labour Party, the English proletarian demand at present is as follows:

CONSTITUTION

Anti-Profiteering Programme

It calls for immediate legislation to effect a drastic reduction in the cost of living in the direct and indirect interests of all bread-winners of the nation, including workers in every profession, civil servants, municipal employees, teachers, salary earners and wage-earners of every class and degree, as well as of persons dependent upon pensions, and small fixed incomes.

Necessities

The Labour Party demands that the supplies of food and other necessities of life (bread, meat, milk, sugar, etc.) water, coal, lighting, and transport-rail steamer, train, and bus, shall be acquired by the State to be administered nationally and municipally, solely in the interests of the public and of the consumers, without profit.

Land

It further demands that nationalization of all land in order to secure adequate dwelling accommodation required for the solution of the housing questions.

Education

All education from primary to technical and university should be free to every citizen able and willing to make use of it.

Diplomacy

It favours the abolition of secret diplomacy, publication of all treaties, the concerted abolition of compulsory military service and standing armaments.

League of Nations

It approves a League of Nations as a practical solution of the problems of war, involving the establishment of international courts of conciliation, of judicial arbitration for the settlement of disputes between nations, and the settling up of an international legislature for the development of international legislation which will definitely bind the contending states. The International System implies Democratic Control of Foreign Policy.

Any one who subscribes to the Constitution and programme (Platform) of the Labour Party is eligible to membership in local labour parties. There are no class lines and the fee is nominal, in some cases only 4 shillings a year; independent of other demands or calls for funds. The Unions as a general rule contribute most of the funds which go to sustain the party and its work.

In the United States there is no political party of large power trying to obtain such ends as the British Labour Party is attempting to secure. But if our people desire these things they should create regular methods.

One advantage of an American labour party (if it were built on the lines of the English Labour Party) would be its comprehensiveness. The British Labour Party consists of the following groups:

The Labour Party is a Federation, consisting of Trade Unions, the Old Independent Labour Party, the Fabian Society, and a large number of Trade Councils (like our American Central Labour unions) and local labour clubs. The Women's Labour League and a Hebrew coöperative society are also affiliated.

There are in round numbers 2,650,675 men, women and youths of working age members of trade unions, and through the unions affiliated with the Labour Party.

The following Socialist parties and groups are affiliated with and accept the decisions in the main of the Labour Party.

National Executive: The Independent Labour Party, known

as "The I. L. P." among Socialists the world over is a pure and simple political organization similar to the Socialist Party of the U. S. with 35,000 dues-paying, red-card members; the British Socialist Party, 10,000 members, the Fabian Society 2140 members. H. G. Wells, G. B. Shaw, Sidney Webb, and Mrs. Webb are members of the Fabian Society.

The Women's Labour League, with nearly 6000 members, and about 2700 co-operatives as previously mentioned, are also affiliated with the Labour Party.

One hundred and fifty Trades Councils (bodies similar to our American Central Labour Unions) and 94 Local Labour Parties (more correctly clubs) are associated with the Labour Party and accept its jurisdiction in parliamentary affairs.

The above figures are not exaggerated but are subject to misinterpretation. To avoid the latter let me state there is much duplication in the membership; men and women who hold membership cards in the I. L. P., the Fabian Society, and the British Socialist Party are members of Trades Unions and through them of course have dual affiliations with the Labour Party. The great majority of the I. L. P. memberships for instance being in the Trades Union movement. In a sense the same may be said of the Women's Labour League, the 100 Labour Parties of the cities (more correctly clubs) all the Trades Council must have Trade Union affiliation. The Fabian Society is perhaps the only body affiliated with the Labour Party which is almost entirely composed of professional people, intellectuals, writers, etc. I would not have gone into such a lengthy and detailed explanation of the groups that go to make up the Labour Party were it not for the seemingly low vote cast for the Labour Party men at the last British general election. Many trade union men have not as yet fully grown used to the Labour Party idea, hence their voting for Tory and Liberal candidates sometimes, especially under the war excitement.

It must be borne in mind that the women members of the Labour Party and in fact of the entire working classes under thirty are ineligible to vote in Parliamentary elections.

The British Labour Party includes many sorts of people and

ideas. It embraces not only the workers but the intellectuals. Such a combination is worthy of notice because in the opinion of Lomonosoff,—the most competent Russian who has visited us since the Revolution—the weakness of the present Russian government consisted in the antagonism of the intellectuals and the workers. Moreover, as the intellectuals are likely to carry on from the past more than do the working classes, the advantage of the intellectual coöperation with labour is not merely the broadening of the group in numbers and experience, but a certain tying of new principles with the economic history of the past. It is worth noting that the history of political science contains no more interesting fact than the fashion in which theory has a tendency under democratic government to be turned into law. Hence again the value of the intellectual.

A Labour Party in America might well expect the coöperation of all liberal groups in a fashion which would promote to some extent internal harmony without uniformity of views, and would make room in the organization of the workers for variety and difference.

The time will come in America when the workingman is persuaded that he has been made a fool of by the dominant parties and will no longer vote with them, just as the time came in England when the working people after the franchise of 1868 and 1885 discovered that the land owner or the manufacturer; the conservative or liberal, liked to have his vote but did not represent him.

In fact, the development of a labour party, which truly does represent labour, is the only way I can see for warding off—at any rate until we can more perfectly understand it—the remoter dangers of syndicalism, which apparently is the coming form of labour organization, both in England and America. We may take all kinds of judicial action against the I. W. W. and editorially call them bad names, but the processes of economic evolution enlarges the field of the I. W. W.

The I. W. W. have organized the unskilled. The unskilled increase as machinery is invented to save the cost of skilled labour. The only form of efficient organization for the unskilled is what is called One Big Union, or "industrial union-ism." Such a union takes in everybody in a given factory or employment and does not divide up into craft unions, which have been called the aristocracy of labor and on the whole have been rather easily handled by the employers.

The mischief of the I. W. W. method of organization is not its theoretical violence but its rejection of political methods. It refuses to be interested in legislation. It is pessimistic about the loyalty of labour leaders who are given conspicuous political places. If our Republic would deal with the labour situation—which an increasing number of the proletariat—namely the I. W. W.—consider outside the possibility of political cure—it should enlarge its constitutional machinery for education and discussion; for political organization and legislation, it should equip itself to meet by efficient political machinery the un-political, so called "direct action" methods that will inevitably confront it.

The complaint is made that the labour party introduces a class distinction into our politics. This is more in word than in reality. Our Constitution itself was the result of party clash and was accomplished on the whole by the party of priv-ilege to such an extent "that the protection of property rights lies at the basis of the Constitution." (See Beard, *Economic Interpretation of the Constitution*, p. 164.)

We of to-day have forgotten the economic struggle before the adoption of the Constitution and the various local revolu-tions such as Shay's Rebellion and the Whiskey Rebellion which this struggle gave rise to.

"In no state apparently had the working class developed a consciousness of a separate interest or an organization that commanded the attention of the politicans of the time. In turning over the hundreds of pages of writings left by eighteenth century thinkers one cannot help being impressed with the fact that the existence and special problems of a working-class, than already sufficiently numerous to form a considerable portion of society, were outside the realm of politics, except in so far as the future power of the proletariat was unforeseen and feared."

(*The Economic Interpretation of the Constitution of the U. S.*, Charles A. Beard, pages 24, 25).

At a time when there are labour parties in Great Britain, in South Africa, and Australia; powerful Socialist parties in France and Italy; when Socialist or international parties are dominating central Europe and Russia, is there a likelihood that America can stem the tide of new ideas and the demands on the part of working-classes in any other way than by admitting the working classes, through constitutional but rapid methods, to a wider participation in the powers of government?

We have in this country the two party system of politics, following England. But England in the last twenty years has gone far from the two party system. A large part of its legislation has been the result of coalition with the Irish Nationalist Party or with the Labour Party. In other words, the group system of legislative control instead of the two party system is the next step that America must take.

THE NEED OF AN AMERICAN LABOUR PARTY

By Mary Kingsbury Simkhovitch

THIS is May Day. Throughout the world the workers are expressing in one way or another their hopes and their purposes. Instinctively the rest of the world reacts either in harmony with these hopes, or in fear of their fulfillment. Many are conscious of a mingled hope and fear, an inner state of perturbation, a sense of confusion. I know a little girl three years old, who for her sins was placed in a room by herself to think it all over. She revolted, and her active mind considered the material at hand for expressing herself. If I should give this Church Congress twenty guesses as to what this child did, I think you will still be guessing. When her mother came into the room half an hour later to see if penitence had taken place, she found her angel child had taken down every thing from the closet and everything from the bureau drawers and placed them in the middle of the room and mixed them all up thoroughly. The child was looking with satisfaction on the heap.

All the ideas and philosophies and customs of men have been taken out of their bureau drawers and mixed in a heap on the floor of life. Or, to put it better, we are ploughed up from the bottom. We have to give a new account of ourselves. We must cease to drift. The world has become more self-conscious and we are really at last beginning to pass from the world of tradition, imitation, custom, habit, into a world of slowly form-ing, inchoate, hesitant purpose. A great land-slide has quietly taken place, a great shift in the balance of human thought and activities. One fact is beginning to come to the surface. One certainty is issuing out of all the haze and uncertainty. This fact is the transfer of power from the few to the many. Mass action is becoming dominant. Infusion of this mass action with coherent purpose is the gigantic task of mankind.

This is a Christian audience and we start together with a fundamental principle which we recognize as valid. No matter how far the Church has wandered from the thought and life of Christ, it still claims to be the extension of His life and still maintains that the essence of that life is love. For the Christian the rule of life is to love utterly. If thine enemy hunger, feed him. Not an eye for an eye and a tooth for a tooth, but love to the enemy, help to the helpless, a complete living into the life of the downmost man. This is the very centre and substance of Christianity—to serve, to love. This is the doctrine of the Cross, the very heart of the atoning life. For the Christian, therefore, the nature of the problem is simple but its execution is as difficult as for any man. But the road we have to travel on is clear.

I was talking with a man the other day whose mind was full of the bitterness of reprisal, whose whole being was centered on the permanent economic overthrow not only of the Central Empire but also the continuance of the economic domination in our own country of the existing classes in power. I asked him how he squared his point of view with the Christian doctrine of love. He said he didn't, that he had reflected on this matter and that he couldn't logically regard himself longer as a Christian. "The Christian philosophy is a dangerous one," he said, "it undermines the existing social order, it presupposes changes too vast to face with anything but dismay."

Here, at least, was honesty. We ought not lightly call ourselves Christians. The Christian way of living was never supposed to be an easy path, and now at the most exciting and turbulent moment in the history of the world, the call of Christ is far more difficult to heed than at any moment in the past. The simplicity and vastness of the claim that we shall love one another perfectly as God loves us is really appalling. To take this seriously as the rule for our social, industrial and national life, to make this great dream come true means such an organization, such a uniting of mankind as staggers our faith and blinds our imagination.   For love can exist only between equals.   Love does not allow of servitude and dependency but implies the mutual service of equals.   Tryanny cannot co-exist with love; and here is where we enter the practical difficulties of our subject.   America fears the tyranny or dictatorship of the proletariat.   Labor fears and proposes to rid itself of the tyranny and dictatorship of capitalistic rule.   But to the Christian all tyranny is hateful.

Of course the word Bolshevism is used in a wholly loose and inaccurate way.   If one of the leading woman patriots in this country can be called a Bolshevist, as she recently was in a leading commercial paper, one really fears for the future of American humour.   Most people mean by Bolshevist the thing they dread most, whatever that is.   Anyone is a Bolshevist who disagrees with one.   I and my group alone are immune.   It needs only the most rudimentary analysis to indicate the childish confusion of mind this term evokes.   Bolshevism has come to mean the synonym for all that men fear.   Now, fear arises chiefly in connection with self-preservation.   What people are afraid of is that what they hold dear will be snatched from them.   People fear death.   They fear the loss of money.   They fear personal attack.   What people want is security, the maintenance of a status satisfactory to themselves.   If people live in an unsatisfactory status, fear is not their primary instinct but the pursuit of the status where satisfactions exist.   In other words, the satisfied want to hang on to their satisfactions and the dissatisfied want to secure them.   And hence exists the natural and inevitable antagonism between those who possess and the dispossessed.   When the word Bolshevist is used, therefore, what is often meant is the fear that what one has is to be taken away.   From this point of view, every increase in inheritance or income tax is confused with Bolshevism.   Every public measure that tends to equalize the distribution of wealth is denounced as Bolshevism.

The Christian, I repeat, is the man who is guided by the law of love, which is the least sentimental and the most practical, but also the most difficult path to follow. To the Christian, the competitive system presents a spectacle of government by force which is intolerable. As one looks about and sees the uncertainties of employment, the maintenance of rentals entirely disproportionate to income, the prevalence of industrial accidents, the carelessness and lack of standard in public hygiene, the whole spectacle of disorganization in our social life—how can men who are efficient in business and women who are able in housekeeping, face this messy, sloppy scene unmoved?

This intolerable situation is certain to be changed. It will be changed either with or without the coöperation of all elements in the community. It will be a community change or a class change. If it is a class change only, it will mean force on one side or the other. Many of the possessing class want to provoke this issue. There are industrial agents-provocateurs at work. At a luncheon the other day I was seated next to a man who bitterly resents industrial change. He said, "I wish they would start something. We'd show 'em." He wished they would start something! He wanted violence for he wanted repression. If it's a question of who is going to get the drop on the other, the odds are in favour of the most powerful group. Is this a road that Christians can follow? No matter how bad our record is, no matter how much we have failed to be brothers, that is still our job—to seek fellowship, to refuse to be tyrannical, to turn the other cheek. Directors and workingmen are our brothers. They must come together. They must work out together the industrial situation. Greater profits must go to labour and an increasing control. Brains and hand must work together with a joint reward and joint responsibility. The Christian social policy is opposed to a competitive capitalistic control on the one side or to a purely proletarian control. Gradually all the people must control all of life with due regard to technical and native abilities. People want control even more than they want wages. Power rather than money is the natural desire of all energetic people.

Now all this is getting recognized. The fine Catholic Labour programme, the programme of the Canadian Methodists, the programme of the Chicago Labour party, of the New York Labour party and the reconstruction programmes of countless religious and social groups throughout the country are all headed in one direction, which may be summed up crudely as the securing of a proper standard of living for all and the increase of dignity of status on the part of the worker. The control of life is what human beings want and what they are entitled to under a democracy which is worthy of that name.

To secure these ends, this growing social purpose has to be incorporated into political action. Where is there proper recognition of this social point of view in political platforms? What have the Republicans to say on this matter? What have the Democrats to say about this?

The fact is that both Republicans and Democrats as party organizations are tacitly committed to maintain the *status quo* of business in this country. The whole system of privilege is safe in the hands of the existing political parties. It is true, this is not the case with the Socialists. But here other factors are predominant. The fact that the Socialist party is largely in the hands of the foreign-born makes a psychological situation unfavorable for a rapid spread of sound democratic industrial ideas and policies. Social democracy would therefore seem to be forced into political action at this time. Yet about this there is naturally a vast difference of opinion. The fate of third parties is not accidental. In it lies a deeper consideration of social psychology. The fact is, a party is not a programme. A party is a group of persons either in or out of power. Parties adopt programmes but pay little attention to them. They come into power not on the merit of a well thought-out programme but on the wave of a popular judgment on one point or at the most two or three. Thus the National Party, so-called, a year or so ago sent around a most excellent (for the most part) document. But no dent was made in public opinion by it. When one or two vast issues are before the public, little attention will be given to well-considered platforms. But while it is true that the party system in our country indicates more a wave or rhythm of popular feeling which now puts in a party and then removes it from power—still it is perfectly understandable that up to the present time, labour has found it wiser not to organize politically. Labour has had to spend its strength in one of two directions, in gaining either economic or political power. It has wisely chosen the former. By standing outside political life it has often wielded the strength of a deciding factor. Labour has been rightly sceptical of political life, but this scepticism has brought about a divorce between our political and economic activity which has given a vantage ground to the direct-actionists, which it is dangerous to emphasize in a democracy. The political and industrial should be welded together. In fact the safety of our political situation depends on the incorporation into it of an industrially democratic programme. If political parties are to be as negligent as they have been in regard to the most important matters of human living, there are only two alternatives open. One is that human living must go on without them—that is, political parties will become negative and our political structure crumble by this very weakness, leaving the actual power outside it; or else, that human life shall be made the very centre and heart of political party action. Unless this is the case, revolution is almost inevitable. How then shall we incorporate our social industrial purpose into political action? Have either the Republicans or the Democrats the nerve to take so great a step? Or are the governing groups of these two parties so made up that they are bound to stay on the defensive? This, I fear, is the case. And it is for this reason that the formation of a Labour party in the immediate future would seem to be inevitable.

Public welfare is undoubtedly the nominal aim of all parties. Republicans have in general sought to show that a protective tariff, the accent on production and prosperity, are synonymous with public welfare. The Democratic party has attempted to show that above all rights stand the right to liberty for the individual, freedom from the repressive measures society may adopt. These fundamental hopes of humanity for economic prosperity and the freedom and liberty of the individual strike down deep into the heart of life. But these aspirations have become so distorted as to be practically meaningless. Economic prosperity is now recognized to be intimately bound up with questions of education and public health upon which it is in the last instance dependent, and liberty of the individual in speech or in the public press would not seem to have been the mark of at least one democratic administration!

Every advance to be truly democratic can have but one aim in view and that is the public welfare. A community programme and community action is what we must seek. For this purpose community organization must take place, not to override or supersede class organization but to include it.

For the interests of employer and employed are not the same interests. It is hypocrisy to claim this. But what is true is that both the interests of employer and the interests of the employed must be subordinated to the interests of the community. The gist of the matter is that from the Christian point of view of brotherhood, mutual service, and co-operation, this country must definitely, purposefully repudiate revolutionary socialism which looks forward to the dictatorship of the proletariat, but that at the same time it must be committed to the deepest and most radical changes in the social structure, which shall substitute co-operation for competition, which shall ensure to the worker a suitable standard of living, and adequate education and an increasing control of industry, till we attain a government which shall be the rule of all, by all, for all.

This ideal of government is implicit in Christianity. It is the meaning of democracy as applied to a world where industrialism is the dominant factor. There is no democracy worthy the name unless there is democracy in industry. Yet although there are a large number of Americans who repudiate the ideals and philosophy and hopes of the early American tradition, and though there are many nominal Christians who do not in the least propose to help establish a Christian social order, I believe there is enough vitality in both Christian and American ideals around which may be rallied public opinion at this time. The crystallization of this point of view is the one important issue of our time. Bishop Brent declared that the British Labour

Party's platform was the one great religious utterance that had come out of the war. Has American Christian democracy no purpose as coherent and definite?

This Congress has the great opportunity to put itself on record as committed to the Christianization of our entire life, working out the social and economic changes in the image of Jesus— substituting co-operation for private profit, and ensuring to every man the opportunity to lead a decent, honourable life where all his powers can be developed and used for the public service.

To attain this end it would seem probable that a political party would be the appropriate means. Yet so deep is the instinct in people to stick by existing institutions, so rightly sceptical are people of new political parties that are likely to prove ephemeral that one can understand the aversion many liberals devoted to a democratic social programme have for this step.

I would venture, in order to meet the objections, many of them compelling, that are offered in opposition to the formation of a new political party, to suggest a modification in plan; a double alignment whereby one might keep one's membership in an existing political party and yet adhere to a new party. We have a precedent for this in the case of the Woman's Suffrage Party which organized thoroughly along political lines and yet allowed membership in an old party at the same time that one became a member of the Suffrage Party. This plan would result in there being republican-labourites or democratic-labourites or plain labourites. In districts where it was obvious the plain labourite could not secure election, efforts would be made to obtain a candidate from the party certain to secure election, and pledge him to membership in the labour party as well. This would line up the labour forces while it would not tie the candidate on certain measures not included in the labour programme. In this case it would be obvious that the labour programme should be extremely simple, centering its accent on these two points of insistence: (1) on securing for all by such measures as may be appropriate a proper American standard of living; and (2) the endorsement of such measures as lead to the greater control of industry by the workers.

The American situation is unlike that of any other country. Yet one may safely say that, broadly speaking, our political fortunes and alignments resemble the English more closely than any other foreign nation. In England while the whole industrial world is seething with change, certain valuable methods and practices are coming into vogue from which we can learn much. The so-called Whitley Councils are not vague matters of pro- gramme; they are matters of fact; they exist; they work. The report on these Industrial Councils ought to be in the hands of the managers of all our industries. They should be studied by all who are engaged in business or who are in any way connected with problems of industrial adjustment.

But Labour will not be satisfied with a shop-steward plan of representation. This is only one step in the process, yet it is a real step. The Industrial Councils open the way for industrial mutual understanding and further joint action.

Here at any rate is a beginning of that important readjust- ment which will have to take place through political and indus- trial action. Industrial group action must be incorporated in the functionings of the state or it will function outside the state. The important—yes, the central—aspect of today's community organization is the furtherance of joint action on the part of all elements in industry for the public welfare.

All our political and industrial action now must be seen in relation to our conception of the nature of government—of the state. The state socialism which was the goal of our radicals so short a time ago is now discarded in the light of the war. The state may be an oppressor of the first order. Only a democratic state can be allowed to take precedence of the individual.

For all government is for the purpose of developing person- ality. The democratic state is the framework within which self-governings groups find their limitations or their fulfilment. It is not a machine that rules the individual. State socialism and autocracy,—these are the very forms of life which we hope we have destroyed. The state is the indispensable co-ordinato of growing forces, holding in check those who would monopolize or destroy life values. Thus the state should never be master of the Church, the Union, the scientific Society, or what not; but rather the framework in which these groups are set.

And yet just as these separate groupings have their own life, so the community as a whole has its life. General policies of public welfare may properly be determined by the community as a whole—the state. But always those policies should be subject to change and held tentatively with due respect to group initiative and technical excellence. Thus the state appropriately conducts public education, but it allows private schools to exist. It insists more and more on public hygiene, but it allows private experimentation in this field. As the community learns to act as a whole on matters relating to the whole, it tends to engage in community enterprises. But only with due regard to private enterprise and to group preferences.

In general, we may be said to be moving in the direction of state-controlled industries or occupations which are necessary for the entire community and at the same time we are considering with increasing confidence the governing of separate functions by the groups immediately concerned.

Guild socialism is the name widely given to this general conception. This trend is opposed both to the enlarged domination of an all-powerful state which would render its members servile and obedient, and equally opposed to the individualistic conception which does not allow for those group relationships which are the real, though often hidden, governing forces of our life.

But all this is a matter of theory. What we have to deal with, as everyday facts, is the grim determination of capital to hang on to private profit at all cost, and also the growing purpose of the workers to control industry.

It is the business of those of us who still call ourselves Christians to apply to this problem our only guide—the law of love. We have the audacity to believe indeed that in us dwells the Undying Fire Wells speaks of and to which the Christian consciousness of all the ages testifies. This Undying Fire, the Spirit of God, the spirit of Love, calls upon us to condemn the violence of capital as we condemn the violence of anarchy. It calls upon us to withstand violence, not by repression—the breeder of violence—but by justice. It calls upon us to put our Christianity into practice by the insistence on a Christian social programme and to this end to make of this Christian consciousness a definite political issue. If we separate religion from politics, we abandon religion.

THE NEED OF AN AMERICAN LABOUR PARTY

By B. Preston Clark

IT is to me a privilege to discuss briefly before you a question of prime interest to us all, and it is a special privilege to discuss it with my friend Mrs. Simkhovitch and with the Rev. Percy Grant, because I am entirely sure that, however much we might differ in methods, the main purpose of our lives is largely the same. There may be differences between us; there can be no antagonism.

In approaching any question, our attitude is apt to be based on certain deep seated beliefs, which have become part of our life and of our thinking. This is peculiarly true of the subject before us tonight. Before we can frame any answer to it, we must go, so far as we are able, to the root of the matter. We must be true radicals. For the true radical is, I think, he who tries to go to the root, rather than he who would pull up the plant, root and all. So I shall try to give my thought on three points.

1. What the nature and the ultimate object of industry is.
2. What the industrial struggle itself really is.
3. What should be one's attitude toward organized labour.

And based on these thoughts:—

1. Is there a need for an American Labour Party?
2. Will it help or hinder the ultimate purpose of industry?
3. Will its formation be in line with those great laws under which at the last we all must live, with the way the world is made?

What then is the nature and the object of industry? A generation ago an industrial unit was conceived of largely as a money making machine, and this had been increasingly true for nearly a hundred years, as modern industrial units grew in size, and as their money making capacity was realized.

The great business men of forty years ago believed that we must build immense industrial machines, and they were built; huge, forceful, and yet necessary, as is every step in the world's progress.

But they met with unexpected obstacles in legislation, that crystallization of public opinion, and in the great labour unions. Many of them broke down on the human side. Sometimes the machines grew bigger than the men who ran them, and they smashed. Natural enough, for after all, the size of any industrial unit is apt to be measured by the length of one man's shadow. Many of them survived and grew in power.

To-day a new conception has arisen. An industrial unit is conceived of by some of us to-day, not as a machine, but as an organism, something alive and growing, with a wise understanding, almost an instinct, for the newer industrial knowledge. This conception of an organism is valuable and suggestive, nor does it mean the elimination of that mangificent genius for individual leadership which has made American business what it is.

For what is the law of life in an organism? Take the human body. The head, the hands, the eyes, *must* recognize each other's value. They bandy no words as to class distinctions; and it is a primary fact of human consciousness that no part of the body, or indeed of any organism, can be damaged without injury to the whole.

I need not make the application to industry, for you will already have made it yourselves. If the industrial unit is in its essence an organism, with mutually interdependent parts, then its ultimate purpose is self evident.

However little in the past this may have been recognized, it is yet true that that purpose *is* the highest development, physical, mental, moral and spiritual, of every person connected with the organization, through the accomplishment by it of its special social function in the most perfect possible way; and also and most important, some fair adjustment of the equities of those within the organization (its management, its workers and its capital) with the equities of the great public which it serves.

Some incredulous spirits may say that this is not an accurate photograph of business to-day in America, and I frankly allow that we are far from the ideal. We in America are wonderful mechanics; we have learned some of the elements of industrial chemistry, but we are just learning the ABCs of the great social chemistry and the human values, through which some day the imagination and the united good will of all the workers will joyfully contribute to the success of a business. It is true that we have yet far to go. But I also submit that we are not the only human activity which still sees its goal far above it. We partly are and wholly hope to be.

My application to industry may sound novel, but in the thought itself there is nothing new. It is as old as the world From the dawn of humanity, to accomplish anything in life, two things have been necessary. There must be the vision. The architect, the sculptor, the statesman, each one of these must have in his heart a picture of the splendid thing he means to create.

But that vision will help the world not at all, so long as it exists in his mind alone. It must be made real in the stone, the wood, the marble.

And in industry the vision of men and women, working happily and gladly under right conditions, at something of use to the world, and in which they are themselves interested; such a vision I say must be made real through such wise humanity and keen intelligence as will result in the business maintaining itself industrially. The game must be played squarely and played hard.

The best human accomplishment always has been and always will be, some vision of truth or beauty, transmuted into golden fact, through hard, sustained effort.

Such is my thought of the essence and the purpose of industry, and so conceived it is of fully equal dignity with any art or with any science.

For while the medium of the artist is wood, stone, marble,

that of industry, rightly conceived, is human nature itself, with its lights and shadows, its heights and depths, its sunlight, its moonlight and its darkness; and always with capacities for the best which we never fully grasp. The uncommon quality of the common man is a constant miracle.

You may say, and you will say with truth, that industry has been, that it is indeed still, thought to be largely concerned with the making of money. But what is happening is this. Dr. Felix Adler saw and stated his conception of industry, which I have largely used, sooner than most of us, yet all over this country today, wise leaders of industry well known that in order to make money they must regard the human factor, that unknown quantity, that X on which so many businesses have suffered shipwreck.

The men of the future see that industry and humanity are inseparable in any successful business, and well it is that this is so. It is as a practical business man that I speak, and not as a theorist. In my judgment human nature is alike the raw material of all industry, its finished product, and the means through which the process takes place.

Now let us turn for a moment to consider what this industrial struggle really is. It has been of course a battle, and in the past, as the history of Trade Unionism shows, it has been too much a battle between classes. Hard fought and with varying fortunes, and resulting today in two enormous forces, organized labour and organized capital, striving, with great waste of effort, like two gigantic tug of war teams.

Here again we must get a new conception, which comes with our increasing democracy. Class lines are being obliterated everywhere. The robber baron has been put out of business by the ballot, the martyrs are no longer tortured, the slave has fought his way to freedom. Freedom, physical, religious, political, is to be the heritage of the world, though more slowly than many of us would wish.

Today the fighting line of this great struggle for freedom is in industry, in the great workshop of the world, where most men and many women spend a large part of their waking hours.

And this struggle, my friends, is *increasingly*, and *because* we are gradually becoming truly democratic, not between the classes. It is between the men and women of every class, who stand for a broad and human sympathy, for a constructive democracy, and those darker hosts who through ignorance or through malice, would set class against class. The cleavage is vertical, not horizontal; and you will bear me out when I say that each one of us today finds allies, and each one of us finds opponents, in our own class, whatever it happens to be, and in every other class. No special group in the community has a monopoly of all the good or all the evil. Human nature as a whole can be trusted. It is the small minority who play the game unfairly who make the trouble for the rest.

To think clear of class and with real democracy, is surely a prime requisite in approaching any human question, and I wonder whether you find this as difficult to do as I do.

To size up a man as a man, independent of those accidents by which our judgment is so apt to be affected, is far from easy. We group people in our thinking habitually. This is natural and proper, but our error lies in our believing this grouping to be fundamental. Employers;—working people;—These are hardly more than catch words. The only human group which is fundamental, the only one to which, when we are at our best, any of us wish to belong, is that which includes all who walk upon two feet.

The ability in our thinking to pass freely over and through the barriers of class is of value, while inability to do so dwarfs and stunts a man's thinking.

This story is not in my paper, but it so well illustrates the limitation of purely class thinking that I must tell it.

A tailor was standing listening to the thunder of Niagara, in the mist that drifts eternally below the horse-shoe falls, and his only remark was, "Great place to sponge a coat." This story is not told at the expense of the tailor. It is told to help myself to remember how easy it is one's self to illustrate the Chinese proverb that "A mouse can drink but his fill from the mightiest river." That one can only get a pint into a pint pot. Or as

Carlyle used to put it, "The eye sees in everything what the eye brings with it the power of seeing." And of the many things that cloud our vision, class thinking is one of the most insidious.

And I am again reminded of a story—

Two men were hoeing in a field in Florida. To them comes running a small boy, excited and out of breath. Says the boy, "There is a man in the marsh over here drowning, won't you come and help get him out?" The men stop and lean on their hoes. One of them asks, "How deep is he in?" and the boy gasps back, "Up to his ankles." The men start hoeing again, one saying, "Oh, he will get out all right by himself." But they quickly drop those same hoes, and run swiftly across the field to the marsh after the boy has said, "Yes, but he's in head first."

It is easy to get into the position of that unfortunate man in approaching the labor question. So be prepared to give me assistance.

Let us turn now from considering the nature and object of industry and the character of the industrial struggle, to organized labour. I approach this subject with a proper caution.

One's attitude toward organized labour must of course influence one's belief or non-belief in our need for an American Labour Party.

I am neither for nor against Organized Labour. I am not indifferent to it. I do not fear it.

Organized Labour exists largely because it has proved a practical expedient by which men could, through collective bargaining, get results in hours, wages, and living conditions, which they had been unable to secure as individuals, and which they would, in a more ideal and human world, have secured as individuals.

I would not wish to see Organized Labour lose anything of that for which it has struggled so long and so hard, nor would I wish to see it weakened until working standards can be maintained by some other means.

On the other hand, a condition like the present, where too

often Labour and Capital are engaged in a gigantic tug of war, means great waste of effort. It is not an ultimate solution, simply a mile stone in the world's history, and a very real and valuable one.

I am in favour of a fair honest day's work, but am against any system which speeds up labor beyond what it can bear, by cutting the piecework rate, by long hours, or by too hard conditions. Equally am I against any system which sets a maximum day's work which shall not be exceeded by anyone.

The best American living conditions must be maintained, and a wage which will make such conditions possible for the workers.

We must have increasing democracy in industry, but we must maintain leadership.

Increasing coöperation between the employers and the workers will I believe point the way towards a condition far better than the present struggle between organized labour and organized capital.

Every employer who treats his employees so fairly, so humanely that they will not feel the need of organizing, will hasten this better day, and every employer who by opposition or hostility (open or covert), to every form of collective bargaining forces them to organize, has his face turned towards the dead past.

Every labour leader who tries with vision to work in coöperation with the best employers, will hasten this better day; and every labour leader, who by thought or act, sets class against class, puts this day back.

In this matter of organization my belief is that if men *are* fairly treated, if the employer knows their desires and their needs, and meets them to the best of his ability, if there are not too many workers, so that he can keep really close to them, they are not apt to organize. In nearly forty years my own men have never organized. And at the same time I should never, and I have never opposed their doing so, should they feel it to their advantage.

Before drawing my conclusions, I wish to say a word of the

time in which we are living. It is a new world, plastic as at the Creation. Someone said the other day, "It is the year One." The war is we hope passing into history. The tumult and the shouting die, the captains, and (very especially) the kings depart. And from this world struggle, two great human facts emerge, like mountain peaks in sunlight, the increasing power of the people and the value of human leadership. As these two powers combine will be the social structure in City, State or Nation; safe, constructive and beneficent, or dangerous and explosive. Either is possible, one of them will most certainly become the reality.

So the real task, the great adventure, is ahead of us. Like old John Paul Jones, we have just begun to fight. And what is it for which this country must work? It is for the same united will in peace which we had in war, and through which we did our part in winning it. Impossible, men say. But America has done the impossible in the past two years, and she will do it again, and yet again. And how shall we get that united will?

Surely through fine leadership, sympathy, coöperation. Coöperation, that factor in Evolution which as Prince Kropotkin has so well shown us, is at the last stronger even than the reign of tooth and claw. You are familiar I know with those wonderful contrasts he draws between the tiger and the reindeer. Between the eagle and the ducks. Between the carnivorous beetle and the bees and ants. In each case the creature which maintains itself by tooth and claw, is a rare creature, it occurs singly. In each case the harmless but coöperative race exists in hundreds, thousands, millions. It may well be that this is one of the lessons of the great war.

Coöperation: its power is colossal. Out of these forty races that throng America, each with its own special and splendid gift to make to the life of this great Nation, there will come such a welding together as the world has never seen. I have that faith. You all have it too.

We are at the last a unit, with a common future and with common problems. On our mutual understanding depends the future of our Nation. United we stand, divided we fall. These people, many of them so untaught, so simple, and many of them of the highest degree of intellect, and all so diverse, are very splendid. They make the bone and sinew of America. As one thinks of our country today, one remembers what Abraham Lincoln said, that God must have loved the common people very much, because he made so many of them.

I know and have always lived close to working people; this has been I think the greatest privilege of my life, and always my faith in them grows stronger. Never have they played me false, and the remembrance of their loyalty and affection is always with me.

My conviction is strong that we do not need an American Labour Party. Such a party would, as I see it, emphasize those class lines, which in industry and in life, we must work clear of. It would not be truly democratic; not in line to produce that united will which we need above all else.

If my conception of an industrial unit is sound; if it is in truth an organism, then in any given concern the common interests of the workers and the employer far outweigh their opposed interests. The old argument used to be that if there were a dollar to divide, there must be a struggle between labour and capital as to the exact number of cents that would go to each. The simile is crude, and lacking in imagination. If you and I are standing on a street corner, and grasped in our joined hands are one hundred coppers, any struggle between us will surely result in some falling into the mud to be recovered with difficulty some perhaps going down the catch basin, not to be recovered at all; net loss to us both. On the other hand, if we use our heads to see what we can *together* do with that dollar, it may easily become $1.10 or $1.25. That dollar may in fact become almost anything. It has the possibilities of fairyland under the magician's wand. And I am not talking fancifully. It is sound practical business. It is what actually happens daily all about us.

So any social alignment in America today, any crystallization, which emphasizes and strengthens class lines, is out of date. It runs counter to the nature of industry itself, as we are beginning to see it, it runs counter to those great tides of democracy against which any of us will put our strength in vain. And it would almost of necessity turn the thoughts of its members too much to the benefits which a single class might gain from industry, instead of leading them to see that the common welfare of all must be our real purpose.

Such a party would simply invite counter-organization, also along class lines. Still the thinking would be horizontal, outworn.

As I see it, what we must work for in industry is a genuine and real joining of forces, a fusing of the best leadership among all the groups, very especially among the business men and the leaders of labour, a tackling of the problems jointly. That sort of effort brings results; it sets forward democracy, without jeopardizing leadership.

We had in Massachusetts a striking example of such a fusing of leadership.

Early in the war there was established a Commission with the Chairman of our State Board of Labour and Industry as its head. Its other members were in equal numbers representatives of labour, and of capital, who before being finally chosen were known to be mutually trusted by one another. The purpose of this Commission was to decide that delicate question, when and how far our Labour Laws should be relaxed during the war, especially as regards the hours and conditions of labour of women and minors. In 547 cases passed on, we did not have one disagreement.

I will go farther, and say that in my judgment wherever class lines are ignored, and management is sound, you will find industrial strength. It has been my privilege to be connected with a mining company operating in Mexico. About ten years ago we went there. We have tried to treat the Mexicans as human beings. We told them that we did not believe the current legend that no Mexican was worth more than two pesos a day, that with us if a man did the work, he would fare just the same, whether he was American or Mexican, that in all ways we should respect them and their wives and families as we would our own. We went to it as a human proposition. The effect was prodigious.

This attitude brought out the best there was in those people, and the best there was in us. For eight years and a half of revolution, under those southern stars, our mines, the roar of our mills have never stopped. Today 7,000 men operate them, of whom 57 only are Americans (less than one per cent).

Mexicans hold important positions all along the line. I could spend an evening telling you that story. How we have fed them, fought typhus and influenza with them, fought everything with them, and how they have done their part like men. Two things I must say. After Vera Cruz we insisted that all our Americans leave Mexico. The properties were left in absolute charge of Mexicans for eight months. They stole nothing; they allowed no one else to steal anything; they operated the plants successfully, and returned them to us in as good condition as when our Americans came out.

On another occasion $250,000 in bullion was stolen from the Company. Our 6,000 miners of their own motion when they heard of this, saw to it that that bullion was returned within twenty four hours, and within 48 hours it was on a Ward Liner bound for Liverpool. Do you wonder that I trust them?

I want to see leaders come out of the ranks of labour as well as from other groups, and I believe this will happen. The fable of the earth giant Antaeus is still true. Strength is at last in the people. But I believe that this is much more likely to happen if the best brains and hearts in industry, the men of vision and humanity, no matter to which group they belong, keep close together, keep in step, and thus learn from one another and learn to trust one another.

Mackenzie King has said that in the past the relations of capital and labour have been those of fear born of mistrust;—that in the future, if industry is to serve humanity, they must become relations of trust inspired by Faith. He further says that the difference between Heathenism and Christianity is that the one is founded on Fear, and the other on Faith. This is worth remembering. It is fundamental. And mutual Faith will not be at all strengthened either by Labour Parties or by Capitalistic parties, or by any parties with class as their basis.

One other thought.   Believing as I do that organized labour as a great conservative force should stand firmly today, I would not like to see them take a position which is more in line with the thinking of a generation ago than with that of the future.

Let me say in closing that these views are not mine alone. Were they so I might hesitate to advance them.   It was my pleasure to sit with Henry Endicott on many of his War Arbitrations, and thus to come into intimate contact with many leaders both of industry and of labour, and the general attitude which I have tried to express to you is, as I have found it, the belief held in common by many of the wisest and most constructive, and let me say, the most successful men of both groups.

PART VI

NECESSARY READJUSTMENTS IN THE TRAINING OF THE MINISTRY

NECESSARY READJUSTMENTS IN THE TRAINING OF THE MINISTRY

By HARRY PEIRCE NICHOLS

THERE is a universal dissatisfaction with present conditions, and a very justifiable dissatisfaction. It is seen in more than a half dozen quarters.

Longsuffering parishes seek ministers; get men that do not meet their needs; lose them if they can; lose, which is far worse, some of their thoughtful and more earnest laymen. Men are in the ministry who ought never to have been ordained; and men are not in the ministry who have a real calling and message, but stay out of it because of what they see.

Rectors are looking for helpers: find candidates in the seminaries complaisantly awaiting bids for their services; discussing fat opportunities with their fellows,—a distinct and lamentable contrast to conditions obtaining in other professions.

Unhappy bishops exist eager to rid themselves of clergy who have been saddled upon them: yet eager to keep vacant posts filled; compelled to care for men canonically resident, and for whom they feel responsible, even to the limit of prevarication.

A consciousness prevails among earnest men, after they have been ordained to the ministry, that they are not equipped to meet the needs of the present generation; that they have wasted the precious time of preparation, been even forced to the waste by existing requirements, on a deal of matter useless for their real ministry. The most unhappy conviction we face in the Christian Church, if we are honest in our look, is the misfits: ministers settled down as incubi incumbents in parishes; ministers in country places when they ought to be in cities; parishes in great cities manned by incompetents;—look candidly at any roster, any convention of metropolitan clergy, look at yourself and the place you are called to fill and the power with which you do not fill it—there, just there, and something must be done for you whether the people hear or whether they forbear.

Seminaries are compelled to do Primary School work, overwhelmed even to exhaustion with petty routine, have neither vision nor time left for more careful or more specialized work.

Examining Chaplains are embarrassed: by dispensations; by duplicated examinations; by requests, even commands, from authorities, to put a man through, to limit his technical examination to twelve verses of St. John's Gospel; and examining chaplains are men, men free to aspire as well as to obey.

Youth, eager to serve their age, turn from the ministry as a place of service to the Young Men's Christian Association; to Settlement Work; to The Red Cross; to many another opportunity to do a man's work for the world of men. The Church with its history, its equipment, its varied ministrations, its conceded value despite limitations and failures, should be alike the best enlistment and the best background for all such human ministries; and it is often chosen as such a platform for good work even by those who regret its antiquatedness. Mature men of proved efficiency in dealing with their fellows are put in classes for examination with striplings just telling what they know of geography and arithmetic; while men tried out and found worthy in the ministry of other communions are set to passing "didomi," and to naming the attendants at the Council of Chalcedon; and men with great and special gifts, whom Harvard would exalt and Rome beatify and canonize, are dumped in one heap with lads merely "passed;" all under the heading "Ordained."

The canons contemplate a beautiful ancient ideal; namely, that it is boys of old church families, known to rector and vestries, stepping from infancy nurtured in the Prayer Book, stage by stage, into the Church's ministry,—though we all know that the Church's ministry is recruited by but a small percentage of these its own children.

In a word our requirements are outgrown, hidebound, inelastic, unchangable, are unjust to men of ripe experience and of consecration. It is not that we want to let down the requirements; rather to lift, to broaden, to adapt them to living needs, to existing and well understood facts.

When we look for the reasons back of this dissatisfaction we find them in the nature of the requirements and in their uniformity.

The requirements for candidacy and ordination certainly as intellectual requirements, have been long left behind. Subjects are required of secondary importance or even of no importance at all,—do not challenge this remark, for it is on such details that theologians fall afoul of each other! More, much more, subjects are omitted which are of prime necessity today. It results, I repeat earnestly, in the time of preparation being exhausted on the secondary; with neither strength nor vision for the more important.

Back of this lies a yet more radical mistake. This is the uniformity of requirements, a uniformity belonging naturally to a simpler time but continued to our own more complex day as if all ministries were alike, a condition now very far from the truth. There is a lack of elasticity in our demands for the ministry and in the characteristics we look for in the men we are training. Lack of elasticity is common and natural in time honoured historic institutions; but the world will not longer tolerate a Rip Van Winkle church.

Now to meet these crying evils, and there are none that cry louder for the Church's heeding to its own good; to face them honestly yet temperately and constructively.

Adjustments are proposed to cover in the widest possible way the demands made by our conditions.

These adjustments have been reached by the deliberations, as a final outcome, and to the credit both of the Church and its constituted representatives by the joint deliberations, of a Commission of both Houses of the General Convention, and of a Council on the Education of Postulants and Candidates for the Ministry named by the General Board of Religious Education. These deliberations have been carried on for the past two and a half years, the Council including seminary professors, examining, chaplains, bishops, and representatives of provinces, meeting some seven times in discussion preliminary to the more official work. It is not too much to assume that you, here present, have followed with intelligent interest the course of this investigation, as it has gone on, and as it has been reported in our Church papers; and that you are now reading eagerly the proposed Revision of the Canons of Ordination on which the Commission and Council have finally and with practical unanimity agreed.

The outstanding points in this proposed revision are:

First: A high Normal Standard for Holy Orders; from which departures are to be made under certain well-defined conditions. It cannot be emphasized too strongly that the plan adopted sets forth as its first note a normal standard to which all conform, a standard as high as one ever held for the ministry, yet adapted to present needs and gauging the increased manifoldness of human interests. The two Plans discussed in the Council and so well known from the pamphlet on "Plans for a Better Equipped Ministry" published two years ago, are not so different in the last analysis; yet they differ radically in what they put to the fore. The one puts to the fore certain well considered carefully outlined requirements, from which departure may be made under certain equally outlined conditions, and with no reflection on any one ordained under the exceptions. This is to say: "Here is the ministry we believe in for the general work of the Church; there is further a ministry we equally believe in for the Church's special needs." The other plan had put to the fore a minimum possible for ordination, on which minumm it is hoped and expected that men will later improve till they measure up to the highest standard cherished by competent authority.

The second point emphasized: Elective Subjects: at least one of which must be offered for ordination. If a Candidate be dispensed from the New Testament in Greek of the Normal Standard, he shall offer at least three Elective Subjects. These suggested, and in part required, electives are a recognition of the existence of exceptional gifts and aptitudes. Ministers are required along many and varied lines hitherto in large measure not formally acknowledged. There should be men in the Church ministry known to be specialists and rejoiced in as such specialists, e. g., in Liturgies, in Music, in Sociology, and as Teachers. Much sport has been made over the list of suggested Electives, amusement ringing its changes on long words, such as Apochryphas, Pseudepigraha; on a man's own "art;" on the study of great literature in its religious application, asking, "What is religious literature?", and being answered, "Carlyle, Emerson, Fiske." For my part I, wish the list were wider, that it took more account of the tremendous difference in man's ability and capacity, that it confessed the value, the essential value, for the work of the Christian ministry, not alone of liberal scholarship, of architecture, of geography, for visions and missions, but of expert knowledge of human literature. Not all ministers to have mastered all these; but in every large community, in every diocese, a man in the Christian ministry to be proud of as an authority on Music as Worship; on the Building of Churches and rectories and parish houses and memorials; on the world's Literature; on the Bible in its original tongues,—a real authority mark you, and not some one who has crammed Greek enough to pass, and neglected the weightier English Bible and the American Church and the conduct of public worship about which he might and should know something worth while.

The third point we stress: The Readjustments formally recognize Special Cases, of which the Church has long been inwardly conscious, whose importance for consideration it increasingly realizes, and whose recognition must be made to meet the duty of the Church today. Thus far there has been a failure to face by the Church as a whole; facts bishops, chaplains, and arch-deacons have been compelled to face; but have been left to face them without advice from the Church, even against the Church's canon law. The result has been hardship, even scandal, as well as needs left unmet. These Special Cases you all know, or recognize as soon as you meet them. They are men of mature age, of realized proficiency and giving promise of usefulness,—their power to deal with men should count as a "subject," a big subject on which they may "pass;" that an examination on such proficiency would be difficult is only a challenge to chaplains, a challenge examiners in our Public School System, presidents in our banks seeking tellers, find ingenious methods of meeting apart from written questions demanding paper and pencils. And there are men of other race and speech to exercise a ministry with their own people. And there are men who "have served with repute and success in the regular ministry of some other body of Christians for at least five years." To treat such Special Cases with special concessions and requirements is due alike to the men and to the work.

The fourth point: A localized Ministry, so named. Places there are to be filled, just as often in our crowded eastern centers and missions stations, as in the new and scattered communities of the broad prairies and mountains of the west—I want to emphasize that this need is as much an eastern need as a western need, and that protest against an "uneducated ministry" is as loud from Montana as from Massachusetts—where men in Holy Orders must be had, and where good and efficient men who have not, at least as yet, conformed to the high Normal Standard may serve acceptably. The danger of the lowering of the standards of the ministry by ordination of men of lesser qualifications, the peril that men press into the ministry from every side under such permission, and ere long flood the whole Church with ordained men, attractive, capable, it may be, but uneducated: it is attempted carefully to guard, by forbidding that a deacon or priest so ordained be transferred from the diocese or district in which he was ordained until and unless the bishop and examining chaplains shall certify he has passed the full standard for Holy Orders. It must be recognized that there is peril in this scheme of permitted ordination lower than the Normal Standard and without the safe-guard of life and experience. Human nature, even in men seeking the ministry, is prone to take the path of least resistance if the gate be ajar.

Vestries are attracted to such men by their success, by their popular ways, by their looks,—vestries may act on secondary considerations as well as—say examining chaplains or bishops. There is more searching of heart on the part of many of us in regard to this proposed Localized Ministry than in the case of any other of the suggested changes. Yet the concession is made to meet an obvious necessity. The demand for such a ministry was insistent. A localized ministry will go to wreck, if wreck it must, on human nature, the human nature of bishops as well as candidates, and may we add, the fallible human nature of parishes and people.

The fifth point: The proposed Canons aim to make plain that all departures from normal requirements rest not on personal dispensing power but on the uniform law of the church. Men are now being ordained, canon or no canon, on different standards, under pressure, by connivance, the excuse being compelling conditions. Our aim is to recognize these conditions, bring them under the law, and thus safeguard the normal and regular.

How then shall we secure the proposed readjustments? How shall we establish the necessary improvements?

We must not propose any radical changes that do not seem required by necessity. Nor is it wise or worth while to propose any that it is practically impossible to put through.

Two features condition success in this big project: an ideal that is worth while, and an ideal that can be secured: an ideal—wise men formulate their wisdom for popular appreciation and approval: its realization—the formulation put through bodies of people mutually jealous of each others' rights. The result has to be attained by concurrent action of the two Houses of the General Convention. This calls for sanctified politics. Nothing was more notable in the idealism of Theodore Roosevelt than his belief in and use of practical politics. He availed himself of party methods, then lifted the party's vision, transcended the party's narrowness. The children of this world are in their generation wiser than the children of light are in theirs. Council and Commission in their omniscience, are prone to forget that their constituency has not studied the subject as they have, do not see with their eyes.

There are three distinct constituencies in this Constitutional Church of ours to be kept amiable in the whole process, to be carried along together not parting cables,—the bishops, the examining chaplains, the standing committees.

The Church's conception of the relation of these three to a well qualified ministry seems to be clear on any fair reading of the canons. Each has an independent yet mutually related and contributive part.

The Bishop, with the man's pastor, stands for the man's general fitness; body, mind and spirit; health, intellectual training, consecration. The Church and the Canon should re-emphasize this duty as first in order. No one in bad health, likely to become almost immediately a burden on the Church; no one without at least a common school education and average intelligence; no one surely without spiritual purpose, good Christain discipleship, should be allowed to get past the first entrance, should be recommended by pastor and laymen to the bishop, or be entered by the bishop on his expectant roll. The place to stop undesirable men is at the beginning, ere they become candidates. Pastors and bishops are too eager to get men into the ministry, are too complaisant in putting their names on the list.

The duty of Examining Chaplains is to test a man on his intellectual preparation: first to study for the ministry at all, then to receive Orders. They inquire into his scholarship, such scholarship as in the judgment of the Church is a desirable test for the ministry. Theirs is a distinctive and invaluable function, to safeguard learning as a requirement for Holy Orders. I am very jealous for the independent and important work ot examining chaplains.

The Standing Committees, presbyters and laymen, advisers of the bishop in behalf of the whole church, equally interested with bishops and with congregations in a pious, sober, and honest ministry. In our democratic order the whole body of the people acts through the Standing Committee. They receive all the required papers and testimonials, pass on their canonical completeness in every particular, act as a final court not of trial but of review.

The proposed Canon, New Canon 6, on Examining Chaplains clearly and definitely states these duties, assigns to each factor in admitting to Holy Orders its honourable part; rather in my judgment makes honourable what before were merely puppet positions. No one of the three, bishop, examining chaplains, standing committee, may act without the other; each and all are necessary for the attainment of Holy Orders in this American Church. Even the General Board of Religious Education, I had hoped to be able to say, of which the Church, having created such an official board to care for so great a subject, has a right to be proud and not leave it with hands empty and folded, may sometime come into recognition in this matter of requirements for Holy Orders, as a valuable advisory body.

It remains between now and the General Convention for the Church; in view of the supreme dignity of the ministry as a determining element of her place and work—in fact the really determining element, for the Church is what the ministry make it, and in view of the terrible unsatisfactoriness of present conditions: First, to realize and visualize the conditions; to recall into vivid consciousness facts simmering already in our minds. Second: to study the plans so carefully prepared for the correction of these conditions with a painstaking and sympathetic study. Third: to discuss; to reach conclusions; to bring pressure of public opinion to bear; to resolve at all costs, with every needed sacrifice, to put through a better way.

It must go through in substance as it is now before the Church, agreed to by such composite and varied constituents as the Commission and the Council. If they buried their differences and preferences and agreed, cannot the Church as a whole reproduce a like harmony? Adopted as a new and radical polcy, it can later be amended from triennium to triennium. As Chief Justice Jay said of the proposed constitution for the United States when it came to New York for ratification, "Let us beware whatever our objections, and no human document is perfect, lest if we reject this we let go an opportunity that will never come again in our time for making a great nation out of feeble and divided colonies." The cause of Theological Education is at stake; it too may be left stranded, and on a shore our ship of the Church may be long in revisiting.

NECESSARY READJUSTMENTS IN THE TRAINING FOR THE MINISTRY AS SEEN BY A SEMINARY ADMINISTRATOR

By GEORGE GRIFFITHS BARTLETT

THE first quarter of the Nineteenth Century, which saw the establishment in this country of our earliest theological seminaries, saw also, in the Churches of England, Ireland, and Wales, a determined effort to raise the standards of admission to the Ministry. In that movement, no one played a larger part than John Jebb, Bishop of Limerick,—with whom, by the way, our own Bishop White corresponded in regard to this matter. "Each succeeding year," Bishop Jebb's biographer tells us, "and each fresh examination, augmented his heart-felt conviction that, in the examinations for holy orders, the best interests of the church, and of religion, were at stake: that TO GUARD THE ENTRANCE OF THE SANCTUARY, was the most effective human security for the welfare of the Church of Christ. In this connection, he often quoted, with cordial approval, an anecdote related of an eminent puritan divine, Dr. Anthony Tuckney, Master of St. John's College, Cambridge, and Regius Professor of Divinity, during the usurpation: one of the first scholars of his day . . . 'In his elections at St. John's, when the President, according to the cant of the times, would call upon him to have regard to the *godly;* the Master answered, no one should have a greater regard to the truly godly than himself; but he was determined to choose none but scholars: adding very wisely . . . They *may* deceive me in their *godliness:* they cannot in their scholarship.'" (Forster's Life of Bishop Jebb (1837) p. 179.)

It is worth while, at this time and in this paper, to emphasize the importance of scholarship.   For there is a shallow criticism current which faults our seminaries and our Canons for their insistence upon intellectual training; and my subsequent argument, as I know by experience, is not unlikely to be misunderstood as playing into the hands of a contention which I deplore. As a matter of fact I am convinced that our present requirements are too low and too yielding.

The reasons for emphasizing sound (though not necessarily profound) scholarship as a cardinal requirement for the Ministry, in all normal cases, are conclusive and permanent.   For, *first*, some dependable test must needs be made of applicants. And, as Dr. Anthony Tuckney shrewdly pointed out, one can test scholarship.   *Second*, to test scholarship is to test character, and test it to the quick.   No brilliant man can become a sound scholar, and no less brilliant man can make steady progress in intellectual attainment, save by faithfulness.   And it is written, not without authority, that "it is required of stewards, that a man be found faithful."   *Third*, it is demonstrably true in all professions, and of all college-bred men, that those in general who succeed in the so-called practical affairs of after life, are those who have succeeded first in their studies: a result that is ascribable partly to the fact already mentioned that scholarship is rooted in character, and partly to the fact that the keen and trained mind is just as necessary in affairs as in bookish pursuits.   I glance over our list of graduates, and I find confirmation of my conviction that in the calling of the Ministry also the most competent student proves the most effective worker. And *finally*, I need not labour, in this presence, the truth that, ideas control conduct, and influence humanity, in the long run, more than anything else; and that therefore great thinking is the most practical of pursuits.   I am aware that original and great thinking is not always synonomous with trained scholarship.   But I do not see that originality or greatness is requisite of the minister.   His business is to appraise thought, to interpret it, to bring it to bear upon the life and conduct of men too hurried to do these things for themselves.   And this, I submit, only the trained mind can do well.   For my part, therefore, I would not abate by one jot or tittle, the intellectual demands of our training for the Ministry.

To say this, however, is not to say that our present training is all it should be. It is my conviction that it deals too exclusively with the concerns of scholarship; that it ought, not by way of substitute, but of supplement, to deal far more with the concerns of life. This is my thesis; and I shall support it from the view-point, not of an examining chaplain, or a parish-priest, but from that of a professional seminary teacher and administrator. My plea, however, is not for revolution, but for readjustment in our curricula. And for this happy phrase, readjustment, I thank the topics committee.

I shall presently give my reasons for holding that readjustment is necessary; and shall attempt to show broadly just what lines this readjustment should, in my judgment, follow. But for the moment I must linger over two or three general considerations.

A. The first of these has to do with the fundamental nature and purpose of the theological seminary. Its primary function, I take it, is, beyond dispute, not to breed theologians or teachers of theology, but to train men for the active work of the Church's ministry, parochial and missionary. I am far from denying that the seminary ought also to produce expert scholars; but this, I submit, is a secondary (albeit a vitally important) function. If this be true, it follows that the seminary training must take account of all the chief factors which are requisite for success in the active ministry. These seem to be four. *First*, the personal life and fitness of the student, in its religious and moral aspects,—yes, even in manners. *Second*, his intellectual training. *Third*, his mastery of professional technique, such as the use of the voice in public speaking, or the art of preaching. *Fourth*, his knowledge of human life and its needs, and of the methods by which religion may be brought to influence life, individual and social, for good. The problem of the seminary is to deal faithfully with all four of these factors,—in such a way as shall give each its due weight. It is a problem, largely, of just proportion. Now the first of these factors,—the spiritual and moral training of the student, must be handled almost entirely apart from the formal curriculum; and I trust that I shall not seem to slight its importance, if in this paper I confine myself to what affects the curriculum proper. My chief point, let me emphasize, is simply that the seminary, existing to train men for ministry, must of necessity keep a just proportion between its training in the pure content of Christian knowledge and its training in the application of this knowledge to human needs; or, in other words, between learning and life.

B. In the second place, the Seminary and Theological Education have had their history; and the conditions we now face are the product of this past. There are three things to notice. *First*, that the norm of our theological curriculum was formulated two, almost three, generations ago. As a matter of fact it has changed comparatively little in all these years, so far at least as the proportions of its disciplines are concerned. *Second*, that since its formulation, both learning and life have changed greatly, even amazingly. *Third*, that, in meeting these changes, our theological seminaries have been hampered by the fact that the Church has not provided the funds for any considerable broadening of their teaching.

I must say a word more particularly on the second and third of these points.

Learning certainly has been revolutionized. Is there one single field of human study, secular or religious, which has not been so transformed that the Scholar of a hundred, or even fifty, years ago would not find himself to-day in an unfamiliar world? Now our seminaries have met and have been equipped to meet this revolution in learning in a fashion that need cause us no shame. Almost from the start we have had our separate endowed professorships in the great staple departments, the Old Testament and the New, History, Liturgics, Dogmatics. The problem here has been one of internal adjustment and growth rather than the provision of additional teachers for additional subjects; and it has been met.

But in the meantime life also has suffered immense change; and with it the task of the minister in the application of religion to life has been revolutionized. Banking, merchandise, medicine, were careers of comparative simplicity in our grandfathers' days; but so also was the work of the parish priest. He then touched life chiefly and influenced it most profoundly, by virtue of his competence in the conduct and ministration of the Church's services and sacraments, and in his careful, scholarly preaching. It is true that he also had some responsibility for Sunday-school work, that he prepared candidates for Confirmation, that he visited his flock, and especially interested himself in the sick and the deserving poor. But contrast this with the demands,—we may like them or not,—which fall upon the parish minister today,—all the business methods of modern life, all the organization, all the pressing contacts with the individual and social needs of the community: set beside these demands, the recognized emergence of new fields of human study, each concerned with the immediate problems of life, and each an attempt to generalize experience for practical guidance, —and you will at once realize the immensity of the change. Psychology is virtually a new science; and the psychology of religious experience is clamouring for recognition. Scientific philanthropy has established itself: it must be reckoned with by one whose calling it is to minister to the sick as well as the whole. Sociology was hardly a name to our grandfathers: it cannot be neglected by the minister to-day, who has come to see that the Gospel which he preaches is essentially a social no less than an individual gospel. Pedagogy has come to its own; and we require by Canon that a Candidate should know something of it. Life, then, as the minister must live it, has grown immensely complex and different; and a whole series of disciplines have arisen, all designed to explain this life and to show men how to better it.

Now the norm of our theological training was crystallized long before these changes came about. And it was adequate then. It gave the minister of seventy-five years ago a really competent mastery of theology; for three years' study then went very much further towards covering that which was known than can three years' study now. It gave him instruction also in all that he had to do in his simple pastoral work,—visiting and confirmation instruction.

Our very endowments still reflect these conditions of long ago. The departments of pure learning indeed have emerged fairly well; for their subjects, as I have remarked, were of independent importance then. But Pastoral Care, as then understood, was too tenuous a subject to demand a specialist's full time. Our founders, therefore, wise and generous in their day, never once established an independent chair of Pastoral Care: if they provided for it specifically, they attached it to something else of more sturdy importance. I, for example, am Jay Cooke, Professor of Homiletics and Pastoral Care. Thus it happens that there is not to-day, in our seminaries from Massachusetts to California, a single teacher whose sole business is to deal with the application of religion to life. We who teach Pastoral Care are invariably academic Pooh-Bahs, annexed to a deanship with all its executive and administrative demands, or forced to spread ourselves thin over one or two or even four additional and distinct subjects of instruction.

Such is the existent situation, and such its historical origin.

C. From these general considerations, let me turn to concrete facts. What relative place in our curricula is given to that aspect of training which deals with religion in action, in application? Here I am confronted by a difficulty of classification which, in fairness, must not be glossed over. Our more purely learned disciplines are, I am persuaded, in the best sense practical: the Study of the Bible, for example. And if I had to choose between Pastoral Care and Holy Scripture as training for the practical minister, I should unhesitatingly choose the latter. Yet the primary and proper function of the teacher in these departments is so manifestly to provide his pupils with adequate knowledge as such,—rather than with methods of using that knowledge,—that I find no perplexity in their classification. But what of Liturgics? What too of Homiletics and of Religious Education? On the whole, however, I cannot feel that these disciplines, with the possible exception of the last mentioned, fall to any prevailing extent into my category of courses in application,—though undoubtedly some fragment of each does so overlap. Roughly speaking, it is under Pastoral Care, in the main, that that teaching which looks to practice rather than to learning, must find lodgement. It becomes germane to our argument, therefore, to ask just what position the department of Pastoral Care holds in the normal curriculum.

Now I have examined the catalogues of five of our representative seminaries; and, naming no names, here are the facts.

In one seminary fourteen courses are necessary for graduation: Pastoral Care is a half course. Thus it claims 1/28 or 3 6/10% of the curriculum.

In another, Pastoral Care and Pedagogy together receive 48 out of some 1304 class hours required during the three academic years. Assume that Pedagogy is given one-third of the forty-eight: then it follows that to Pastoral Care proper there fall thirty-two hours,—or 2 4/10% of the whole.

In a third, the full training requires 1311 class-room hours: twenty-eight of which are assigned to Pastoral Care; or about 2 1/10% of the whole.

In yet a fourth, Pastoral Care is allotted thirty-one class hours, out of a total of 1536; or a trifle less than 2% of the total.

Finally, not to spare my own glass house, our Philadelphia seminary requires forty-eight units of work for graduation, and my course in Pastoral Care is valued as one unit: again a trifle over 2% of the whole.

I reach the conclusion, therefore, that our Seminaries to-day devote only from 2 to 3½% of their teaching time to Pastoral Care. Add to this, in all fairness, Religious Education, and some relevant portions of Liturgics and Homiletics; yet still it is hardly probable that more than 5 or at most 6% of our training time is given to instruction in the methods of applying religion to life, or to the conditions and needs of that life, individual and social, which it exists to redeem. This, I submit, is a faulty, a gravely faulty, emphasis.

D. I notice yet another fact which appears to me significant and sinister. There is literally no developed modern literature of Pastoral Care. The teacher in this department is not only without adequate text-books; he is also unable to assign adequate collateral reading. There are indeed excellent books on social service, though for the most part they deal with principles rather than application; and still finer studies of social conditions in town and country, some of them written with an adequate sense of the religious problems involved. There are many books on the dependent, the defective and the delinquent classes, and on the methods of modern philanthropy. There is a growing literature in the psychology of religious experience; and a large literature on pedagogy,—even from the distinctively religious point of view. And of course there are noble books of inspiration dealing with the personal life of the priest. I find occasional use also for one or two general books, such as Dean DeWitt's "Decently and in Order," and Dr. Washington Gladden's "The Christian Pastor and the Working Church"; and I refer my students to many volumes on particular topics of detail such as Dean Hodges' study of the Institutional Church. But I know of one, and only one, really masterly treatise on the art or science of Pastoral Theology; and that one is but prolegomena,—a first mapping out of the ground a treatise should cover, and an attempt to define the methods it should pursue. I am alluding here to Prof. Clement F. Rogers' invaluable "Introduction to the Study of Pastoral Theology." But there will not be any vital and satisfactory practical training to our students, till there be a literature of the subject,— till the immense but scattered results of personal experience in the ministry to mankind, be correlated and digested. Nor will this be done till there be men to do it, fitly chosen, and enabled to give their lives as specialists to the task.

Such is the situation as I see it. The question remains: what should be done by way of amendment? I would urge three steps: *first*, the gradual formulation of a wise articulated scheme for this training in the application of religion to life; *second*, the demand for endowments adequate to secure the proper teaching staff; and *third*, the provision of a fourth year in the seminary course, so that this practical training may be given on a useful scale, and yet without supplanting the immensely important subjects already dominant in our curriculum. With a few words, on these points, I must end my paper.

1. *The Need of an Articulated Plan for Practical Training*

I question whether we are ready yet to formulate a plan for the adequate broadening of the practical side of our training: certainly *I* do not feel competent to do so. I can, and presently I shall, name certain subjects which I consider rather likely claimants for admission. But I suspect that the development of Pastoral Theology, in the broad sense, will involve not a little experimenting, and very likely some mistakes. There are, however, a few general considerations which I find myself increasingly disposed to regard as formative, in any attempts to plot out a satisfactory scheme.

(a) In the first place, I believe that the principle of specialization must have rather free play. The intellectual training we give, in Holy Scripture, Dogmatics, History, and the like, is, I think, quite fundamental for all our students, whatever their after work may be. And, undoubtedly, what we now give of Pastoral Care, and even more, would prove "generally necessary for salvation." But beyond this, specialization ought to come in. And this would involve the provision of a considerable range of elective courses.

(b) In the second place, the teaching in this department must subserve two main ends: it must be descriptive, in the best sense,—bringing the student in some way or other into closer intimacy with conditions as they are; and it must be methodological,—teaching him how to deal, as a minister of the Gospel, with these conditions.

(c) In the third place, mere lectures and class-room instruction alone will not suffice: the seminary must find means of reaching out into the surrounding world, and of carrying on a kind of laboratory work.

(d) In the fourth place, some of the courses I have in mind could obviously be given by the university as well as, if not better than, by the seminary. And there are strong reasons for such close affiliation with the university. Yet I am persuaded that it would be a capital mistake wholly to dissociate this human nature aspect of the training from the seminary proper. That "*nihil humanum sibi alienum est*," is a cardinal truth of Christianity; and I have the strong feeling that both our seminaries and the Church they serve seem to men, and really are, somewhat restricted and remote from actualities. The disciplines I urge, if made part of the inner life and being of the seminary, would help it to see life steadily and to see it whole.

(e) Finally, I am more and more inclined to feel that from one-fifth to one-fourth of the average student's time should be given to this aspect of his training.

And now let me specify some of the courses and types of courses which, in my judgment, deserve serious consideration.

(i) *Current Church Problems*

Our students go out as leaders, with no trained understanding of the larger problems before the Church,—such matters as are discussed by the General Convention. I am thinking of Reunion, the Racial Episcopate, Marriage and Divorce, the function of Provinces, and the like. We sadly need a public opinion in the Church which would face these larger issues with statesmanlike intelligence. And to get it, we must begin with our seminary students.

(ii) *The Psychology of Religious Experience*

There ought to be a course, or courses, in the psychology of religious experience. By this I do not mean that Psychology of Religion which attempts to fathom the origin of the religious sense, and to study comparatively the primitive forms of religion,—but the study of the religious nature and reactions of contemporary humanity. Those who have read William James's "Varieties of Religious Experience," or Coe's "The Spiritual Life," or Davenport's "Primitive Traits in Religious

Revivals," will understand what I mean, and will, I think agree that though this subject is still in its infancy it has promise of great usefulness.

(iii) *Descriptive Courses in Social Conditions*

There has been nothing finer in the literary output of the last thirty years, than the large number of intensely vital books, which like Jacob Riis's pioneer effort, show us "how the other half lives." Cross sections of actual life these give us. And out of their study there can and should grow up specialized courses in the methods of Church work in certain well-defined classes of communities: industrial and urban, agricultural and rural.

(iv) *The Dependent and Delinquent Classes* should be studied; for the Church of Jesus Christ has a special ministry to the outcasts of society.

(v) *Courses in Social Theory*

To these descriptive courses there should be added one or more courses in social theory. For nothing more needs a Christian solution than the urgent, the supremely urgent problem of the reconstruction of our present social and industrial order. And if the Church exists to bring in the Kingdom of God, this task dare not be shirked.

(vi) *Laboratory Courses*

The subjects I have just mentioned could be handled mainly in lecture courses. But there is need also of training which should be more in the nature of laboratory work. It is often argued, I know, that in the training of the ministry you cannot duplicate the clinical practice of the medical and the dental student,—for you cannot take your pupil with you to the bedside of a sin-sick soul. If that were *all* the duty of the minister, the objection might hold. But in reality it is supremely shallow, and is based on the pernicious heresy that Christianity concerns individuals only. Is there any reason why our students should not be trained in Sunday-school teaching and management in a model Sunday-school,—whose superintendent should be a member of the faculty? Or why our city seminaries should not build up working alliances with the City Mission, the Rescue Missions, the Society for Organizing Charity, and the like,—through which definite experience might be gained under expert guidance? Or why our country seminaries,—or for that matter our city seminaries too,—should not serve a circuit of rural missions, placing a priest in charge who, as a member of the faculty, should oversee and instruct the student lay-readers? All, or almost all, the necessary elements for the up-building of such a system of practical training seem to me ready to our hand. What is needed is money for maintenance; and a touch of constructive imagination and daring on the part of seminary and of diocesan authorities—and the thing could be begun to-morrow.

(vii) Finally, I must not fail to mention the need of special courses for those who are preparing for missionary work at home and abroad; though I may not pause to develop the suggestion. And not least of all, I would urge strongly one or more courses which should treat the English Bible from the standpoint of Pastoral Care. E. g., I give an elective course based upon the four Gospels, which attempts to study our Lord's methods in the training of the Twelve, and the principles of His own pastoral work among men: I have found it, and I think my students have found it, fruitful.

2. *Endowments*

That all this would require substantial addition to our endowments is obvious. I cannot count this a valid objection,—though a very present difficulty it is. For I have never been able to persuade myself that its cheapness and not its effectiveness was the proper criterion of a seminary education. Once let the Church realize that a better training can be given; and it will, I firmly believe, provide the means. Besides, the development need not be quite as costly as it looks. It is possible, at least, that some of these subjects might be taught by a single expert in two or even three seminaries. It is possible that closer relations with the great universities might care adequately for others. Nor is it necessary that all our seminaries should teach all subjects: a system of specializing might be worked out with advantage for institutions no less than for their students.

3. *A Fourth Year*

I have said repeatedly that my hope is to see this development of Pastoral Care provided as a supplement to, not as a substitute for, our present work. There is only one way, I take it, by which this is possible: to add a fourth year to our period of training. I must not elaborate this point, at the fag-end of an over-long paper. The change is coming, I believe, as surely as it has come in the great medical schools; and it is as necessary.

The fourth year would give the student a chance for genuine practical training,—would do what our diaconate is in theory supposed to do. And in the comparatively few cases where it was clear that the individual student's true function in life would be to serve God as a scholar, the fourth year could be utilized for specialization in learning rather than in practice. Thus, every way, the change would be great gain.

Such is the readjustment which I believe necessary in our training of the Ministry. I leave it to your judgment, with but this final word.

I am impressed, in my own experience with the average student, by frequent evidence of a failure on his part to grasp the significance of the training we offer him. It is not wholly his fault. He comes, sometimes, with sincere yet narrow and even grotesque conceptions of the life-work before him. Or his conception, if deep and devoted, is too little intelligent. And over against it we set perhaps too unvarying a discipline of would-be exact learning. We insist upon the facts of history, the results of Biblical criticism, the niceties of Greek grammar, the elaborations of doctrine; and very little else: what have these things, the student asks, to do with the functions of the minister, in Hankow or Alaska, in the teeming metropolis or the quiet country? Much every way, in reality. But our seminary course, by its sheer inadequacy in those departments which obviously bear upon life and reveal religion as a power in action, gives the impression that the whole course, and the whole career for which it prepares, is cold and theoretical and impractical. Change this, by a vigorous infiltration of those living subjects which I have pleaded for, and you change the quality and the tone of the whole period of preparation. It will gain a better focus, a truer balance, a clearer objective, and consequently a deeper consecration. Its pure learning will gain in self-evident importance, when thus set in a more just perspective. And the course as a whole will be aiming, with an effective adjustment of means to ends, at the one supreme goal, the establishment of the Kingdom of God, on earth as it is in heaven,—the greatest of all practical objects. Slowly, but surely, we have come to see that the old objective of individual salvation must be,—not abandoned, God forbid,—but crowned and completed by the objective of social redemption. Slowly too, we are recognizing that our old religious methods are inadequate to the new task: that our sacraments and services, our preaching and our visitation of the sick and the afflicted, immensely potent though they are for good among those who are already securely within our influence, do not, alone, avail to bring the seething mass of humanity into that obedience whence only can spring man's peace and God's righteousness on earth. Thus the new vision is as yet imperfect; we see the haven where we would be, but we know not by what paths or by what methods to reach it. And yet it is man's special part, in that great redemptive work in which God and man are co-partners, to deal with application, to build up an intelligent, coherent, adequate body of methods,— and then to use them. It is high time that we were newly about this business, with all our heart, and all our soul, and all our mind. And the place to begin is in the training schools of the ministry; and, within them, in the departments of Pastoral Care.

NECESSARY READJUSTMENTS IN THE TRAINING OF THE MINISTRY

By Edward Staples Drown

I ASKED a clergyman what he thought to be necessary readjustments in the training of the ministry, and he said, "The first thing is to teach the student how to raise money." I do not suppose that the answer was to be taken seriously, but it raises the whole question as to what kind of a ministry the Church wants. If the minister is to be primarily an expert money raiser, then the theological school should be turned into a business college. If the Church wants the minister to be a universal expert in political and social and hygienic reforms, then the theological school should become a school of political and social science, supplemented by a medical department.

I don't want to be misunderstood. The minister must of course be vitally interested in social reforms. But such matters are equally the business of every citizen, especially of every Christian citizen. But they are not the distinctive business of the minister. The minister cannot claim to be an expert in all modern social problems. I once saw a physician's sign which read, "Specialist in acute and chronic diseases." We rightly distrust the universal specialist. If the minister claims to be an expert in every department of modern social life, he will arouse only the contempt or the pity of those who know.

I assume that this is not the ideal of the Christian ministry. Yet the ideal is of no less social value than that which is here presented. The Church demands a new world of righteousness and truth. But it believes that that new world must come down from God out of heaven, that it must be the creation of Him who said, "Behold, I make all things new." We may well recall the reputed saying of Archimedes, "Give me a place to stand, and I will move the world." The business of the minister is to lead the Church in moving the world, and his standing place, his ποῦ στῶ is faith in God the Father and Creator of life, in God the Son, incarnate in humanity, in God the Holy Ghost, the true source of human fellowship. The distinctive purpose of the Christian ministry stands or falls with the belief in God as the creative source of a new world.

This position follows from the essential character of the Christian faith. The higher religions of the world have been classified as religions of "culture" and as religions of "redemption." By a religion of culture is meant a religion that maintains and guards a certain condition of society. It preserves the *status quo*. But such religions contain no principle of progress. As society develops, the religion becomes antiquated. A religion of redemption, on the other hand, reveals the contents of the life of God, as beyond and above the world. Such religions are not satisfied with the *status quo*. They demand something above this world, they believe that only in the unseen can be found the true satisfactions of life. But their danger is that they draw the worshipper apart from life, that they underrate the importance of this world in the interest of the world to come. The true religion must unite the two worlds. Drawing its power from the world above, it must continually express that power in the world that is here and now. And that is the very essence of the Christian faith. It is the union of the religion of redemption and the religion of culture. Its kingdom is not *of* this world, but it always seeks to transform the kingdom of this world into the kingdom of our Lord and of His Christ.

If this be true, then the minister must above all be a man of faith, of faith in God as the source of human unity. Hence the training of the ministry. My contention is a simple one; the primary and fundamental study in preparation for the ministry should be the study of theology.

It would seem as though that ought to go without saying. Did not Artemus Ward in writing for *Punch* excuse himself for joking, by saying that it had always seemed to him to be proper for a comic paper to have an occasional joke in it? Yet, if we judge by the popular demand, theology would seem to be the last thing wanted in a theological school. It is contended that the minister should be practical rather than theoretical, ethical rather than theological, apparently a man of the people rather than a man of God. These objections prove my point, for they indicate how totally inadequate is the general idea of what theology is. Christian theology deals with the knowledge of God as He is revealed in Jesus Christ. And God the Father of our Lord Jesus Christ is the source of all that is best and truest in human life. God is the Creator and Father of men, and men are made in the image of God. It is a principle of all true Christian theology that there is no truth about God which is not capable of expression in the life of man. Every Christian doctrine, every dogma, about God must by that very fact be a doctrine or dogma about man who is the son of God. "If a man say, I love God, and hateth his brother, he is a liar." That is the principle of a Christian theology. The belief in the kingdom of God is the most radical, the most revolutionary of all social concepts. It overthrows the divine right of kings by the divine right of every child of God. The belief in Christ as King of kings, and Lord of lords hath put down princes from their thrones, and hath exalted them of low degree. Only on that foundation shall the government of the people, by the people, for the people not perish from the earth.

In pleading for the study of theology, I am therefore not pleading for a "stand pat" attitude. We need radical readjustments in the training of the ministry. But those readjustments do not so much demand new subjects as a searching and radical readjustment of old subjects. We need to bring out the ever new resources of the Christian faith. That Christianity is the absolute religion does not mean that it is static. Its absoluteness is its capacity for eternal progress. That Jesus Christ is the same yesterday and today and forever means that He is the Man for every age, the giver of the Spirit who shall guide us into all truth. If the ministry is to do its work today it must searchingly apply Christian truth to the needs and problems of our own time.

The theology needed in the preparation of the ministry must then have two marks which need only to be mentioned. First, it must be true, radically true, to the essential Christian principle, and to its productive power. Secondly, it must be brought to bear on life, it must be spoken in a tongue understood of the people. With those two marks in mind, I proceed to the application of the principles that I have been considering to the theological curriculum.

In the multiplicity of demands on the ministry today, of course no single curriculum, no prescribed course of study, can meet every need. There must be large and probably increasing opportunity for election of subjects. Especially must be borne in mind the distinction between the needs of the technical scholar in the ministry, and the needs of the ordinary man. There is great need of fine scholarship. The Church will suffer tragic loss if it does not have real scholars, and that not only as writers of books, and in theological chairs, but in the active work of the regular ministry. Lack of sound scholarship has time and again held back the Church from success, and has kept it from meeting new issues as they arose. Take, for example, the two great advances of the last century, in science and in Biblical criticism. Now that the results of science and criticism are accepted, we can see that the lack of sound scholarship made for the Church unnecessary foes. Only deep and broad scholarship can prevent such unfortunate results. We may well remember the difference between strategy and tactics. If the ministry is trained only in tactics, only for immediate results, it will fail to meet the larger issues as they arise. Only by strategy, by a far more comprehensive grasp of fundamental issues, the immediate application of which may not be clearly seen, will the Church win its true victories.

> No end to learning:
> Earn the means first—God surely will contrive
> Use for our earning.

....

> Oh, if we draw a circle premature,
>   Heedless of far gain,
> Greedy for quick returns of profit, sure
>   Bad is our bargain!

Searching scholarship will always be needed, and the theological school must in every department provide ample facility and incentive for the thorough scholar.

But real scholars are rare. Many men must be content with results arrived at by others. The school must equip such men in a practical way for effective work in the ministry. The larger number of students will be of this class, and any suggestion for a theological curriculum must bear in mind the distinction between the needs of the technical scholar and those of the average minister.

In maintaining that theology is the most important subject, I do not mean to limit theology to Christian doctrine and its immediately allied subjects, fundamentally and supremely important as I think those to be. For these subjects are, of course, vitally connected with knowledge of the Bible and of Church history, and must also have their immediate outcome in practical theology. The old and well established division of theology into the four departments of Biblical, Ecclesiastical, Systematic, and Practical, will serve the purpose well enough, if the content of each department is duly appreciated. I proceed to a few suggestions under each of these heads.

First and foremost there must be a thorough knowledge of the Bible. How that should be acquired depends on whether the student is to be trained for technical scholarship or not. The Biblical scholar must know Hebrew. But for the average man Hebrew should be an elective. The accepted results of Old Testament criticism can be taught without Hebrew, and, with the demands upon the ministry today, Hebrew, imperfectly learned and perfectly forgotten, is a waste of time. With Greek the case is different. If we could get hold of the future minister as a boy and superintend his course through college, we ought certainly to make him learn Greek. But many men, probably a large majority, do not decide on the ministry until their college course is nearly or fully ended, and many of these know no Greek. We are confronted "with a condition, not a theory." Is it worth while for such men to learn a very little Greek during the precious and crowded hours of the theological course? I believe not. And, although I feel as if I were standing by the grave of a dear friend, I reluctantly conclude that from such men Greek should not be required. A professor in Princeton Theological Seminary once opened his class with the prayer, "We beseech thee, O Lord, that thou wilt keep thy Church from the disgrace of having a ministry which cannot read thy Scriptures in the original tongues." One would like to say Amen. But the time has passed.

It is not necessary to discuss details as to the study of the Old and New Testaments. The student must meet the full results of honest and fearless scholarship. Without those results the Bible may today become a stumbling block to faith. Every minister, whether a technical scholar or not, ought to be able so to handle the Bible as to make free the word of God, unhampered by theories which have been and are hindrances instead of helps. There must be cultivated the sense for honest exegesis, a resolute resolve to find the meaning of the written word, unbiased by our own theories or theologies. The Old Testament must be taught as the record of God's growing revelation in the life of man, through the sacredness of the family and of the nation, the means by which the righteous God is revealed in the just relations of man to man. The New Testament must give us the living Christ, the supreme revelation of God, the center of human unity, the foundation of the Church, which is the forecast and the sacrament of the kingdom of God on earth. But all this, and much more, should go without saying. The Bible is the starting point for a sound theology and for a right conception of human fellowship.

In regard to Church History and the history of doctrine, the readjustment necessary is again not in a change of subject. It is the adjustment to the needs of the ministry today. Every provision should be made for the work of the real scholar. For the average student there must be a good knowledge of the general history of the Church, and a special knowledge of the heritage which comes through our own branch of the Church. Here the need is especially great in view of the pressing problem of Christian unity. Whether the subject of Ecclesastical Polity is studied under Church history or under some other head, is of small importance. Vitally important is it that the student should understand the historical attitude of our Church and of the Church of England, its sanity and breadth, its lack of narrowing negations. There are fantastic theories abroad as to the position of our Church in regard to the ministry and in regard to other Churches. They can be met only by a sound knowledge of history. Would that the student should be acquainted with the breadth both of the churchmanship and the statesmanship of the judicious Hooker! So trained he would present our Church as contributing to Christian unity rather than to sectarian narrowness.

We come now to the field of theology in the more limited sense, that is Systematic Theology. The established division into Apologetics, Doctrine or Dogmatics, and Ethics, will serve well enough as a convenient classification. The readjustment must come in the way in which these subjects are treated. Apologetic problems must necessarily be prominent. Men are asking the most fundamental questions, and they must be answered. But the old fashioned method of treating apologetics and Christian evidences will no longer serve. The whole subject may perhaps better be treated as the philosophy of religion, including not only the psychology of religion, but also some study of ethnic religions and their relation to the Christian faith.

More important even than apologetics, however well treated, is, I believe, the subject of Christian Doctrine itself. For the best apologetic will come from inside, not from outside. Here we need the most searching readjustment and restatement of Christian theology in the terms of life today. To make such restatement is the task of theology in every age. Every great period of theology has been a progressive one, for every true theology has spoken for its own time. "David, after he had served his own generation by the will of God, fell on sleep, and was laid unto his fathers." If a theology has served its own generation, it must be content to fall on sleep. The theologian of today should know the theology of the past, but in order that it should help him to serve the present. Theology must be ever new, as it is not content with results that are laid unto the fathers, but seeks the living seed that shall ever bring forth fresh and living fruit.

And herein must be the best Apologetics. What is needed to convince men of the truth of God in Christ is not so much an outward apologetic approach, as a vital unfolding of its contents and of its value for life. And here I repeat that the chief training for the minister must be in theology, the attempt to understand the ways of God and to make those ways plain to men. Men are hungering and thirsting after God, and unless the Church can know God and can interpret Him to men it will fail in its mission to our time. No amount of social schemes, no expert training in details of social problems, can supply the lack of the knowledge of God, who is the source of human unity and the foundation of social righteousness and peace.

Theology must therefore pass into Ethics. Indeed the Christian ethics is not so much a different subject as it is the expression of the life of God in the life of man. All true theology must be social, as all true ethics are social. The minister if he be a true theologian must have a passion for social righteousness. Otherwise he has no vision of God. That vision must lead him to demand the essential rights of man. The Christian ethics, founded on the belief in God, must lead the student to seek the foundation of a society that shall establish judgment and truth. And that society is the kingdom of God.

The last general department, that of Practical Theology, demands probably the greatest number of changes, not only in treatment, but in subjects. Naturally, such established subjects as Homiletics and Pastoral Care will remain essentially the same, the readjustment being in new methods of treatment. But in certain respects the department must develop along lines that have so far been imperfectly treated. And in many respects the treatment should vary according to whether the student is planning for the work of the ordinary parish minister, or whether he intends to specialize in some particular field.

Quite fundamental should be the emphasis on Christian education. Good work has been done in methods of teaching, child psychology, and the like. But the problem is a bigger one. All our war chaplains seem to agree that Protestant Christianity has failed in educating its boys. They say that the men in the army know almost nothing about the Christian religion. Certainly they lack definite knowledge. The *Ecclesia Docens* has failed to do its work. Here is an enormous task that demands the best attention of our best men.

A new extension is also required in the field of social service. The demand is insistent, and at present presents more problems than solutions. Certainly, as said before, the minister cannot claim to be an expert in all social questions. But he must be in deep sympathy with them, and must be in intelligent touch with the means being worked out for their solution. And, however difficult the solution, the problem is clear; it is to apply the Christian law of justice and service and love to industry, to the Nation, and between the Nations. And in all the difficulties we may well remember the noble saying of Kant, "Thou oughtest, therefore thou canst."

Full provision should also be made for those who plan to devote their ministry to special fields, such as rural work, labour, immigration, and the like. To be sure there is a difficulty here. It is seldom possible for the student to determine definitely where his work will lie. Much will depend on future circumstances. It might be an excellent thing to have a special course for the training of bishops. But few theologues would venture to elect it. An Armenian student once consulted me as to whether he should be married or be a bishop. But few of us can make beforehand such a definite choice. Perhaps the way out will be to provide graduate courses for men whose work has already been determined. And different theological schools may well specialize on particular kinds of such graduate work, thus providing better facilities, and avoiding reduplication. There is here large opportunity for future development.

I need hardly mention the necessity of the problem of Missions. In addition to the instruction that every student should have, there must be special work for those who have already determined on the mission field. This should include not only the study of missionary methods, but also the relation of the Christian faith to other religions, especially those of the country to which the student expects to go. Here again special schools may well do special work, provided that every school has that missionary motive without which no school is Christian.

There is one other subject which I hardly know how to name, but which is of the utmost importance. I may call it a knowledge of human nature, leading to the ability to understand and deal with men and women. How, if at all, it can be taught, is the problem. I do not believe that any development of the study of casuistry as a training for the confessional will be helpful for American Christianity. Some expect much help from psychology. It may come in time, but modern psychology is a new science, and for a long time to come I fear that its results will not become truly practical. I recently heard it said that the Germans know more about psychology and less about human nature than any people on earth. We can hardly expect a chair of Human Nature, but that is what is needed. The student should read good literature, including the drama and the novel. He should read newspapers and magazines. Above all he should be a Christian gentleman. And a gentleman is a thorough democrat, who is at ease among all sorts and conditions of men, and expresses himself to them without awkwardness and without fear.

This requirement reminds us that the theological course as such cannot complete the training for the ministry. A large part of its practical side must be acquired in the actual experience of the cure of souls. Any theological school that thinks it can turn out a finished product had better close its doors at once. It is a vain pretence. What a school can and should do is to lay deep the foundation on which an efficient ministry can be built.

It is therefore of vital importance that the student should in his theological course learn those things which he is not likely to learn elsewhere, and that he should give little time in the school to those things which are sure to be learned through the manifold experiences of the priest and pastor. The legitimate demand that the theological course should be practical must not degenerate into the notion that the theologue should practice a dilettante ministry before his time. Phillips Brooks used to say to students: "Do not be in a hurry to get out into your ministry. The world can wait for you. It has waited a great many hundred years for you already, and it can wait a little longer." The most practical results can best be reached on the broadest and deepest foundations. By building these the school will best do its duty to the Church.

What means can be used to promote these necessary readjustments in the training of the ministry? Little can be done by canons of the general Church. The canons to be presented to the next General Convention are a great improvement on our present ones, and I trust that they will be adopted. But canons can no more produce an educated ministry than laws can produce righteousness, and we are all too good Protestants to believe that. Much will depend on how canons are administered, and in any case it is an easy thing to cram or to be crammed to pass examinations. The theological education needed cannot be produced by legislation.

That is indeed a fortunate fact. The last thing wanted is a uniform system of theological education. Such a system is sure to be limited and is apt to have most of the deficiencies and few of the excellencies that belong to contributions from varied sources. The world today is too complex for anyone to see it clearly and see it whole. Perhaps no man of the present generation has seen it with perfect clearness except the Kaiser, and it is probable that even he has recognized that certain elements of it have escaped his observation. With great seriousness I mean that any attempt to codify or unify the education of the ministry will be sure to do injustice to the enormous tasks that press on us today.

If those tasks are to be adequately fulfilled they must be fulfilled by diversity and not by uniformity. And here comes in the value of separate, distinct, independent theological schools, and of the special contribution that each should bring to the wholeness of truth. Our schools should be different from each other. What is needed is that each one develop its own gift. There should be no jealousy, and the only rivalry should be rivalry in doing well the work of Christ.

Only thus can we get the freedom and win the development which the Church so sorely needs. I heard the late Professor Nash once say that the trouble with the Episcopal Church is not that it is over-sparred, but that it is over-ballasted. We run no danger of an upset. Any one who is in a panic on account of the unsettled condition of the Church is raising bogies out of his own fears or his own lack of faith. We *need* to be unsettled. The Church will not capsize, but it is in serious danger of slow progress. The times are new, and they call the Church to new ventures and new dangers. God forbid it should be written of her that standing on the borders of the new land she could not enter in because of unbelief. And such unbelief means lack of courage, or, as it has been well said, lack of great-heartedness. We need that in various centers of the Church's thought there should be honest, fearless, searching scholarship, a resolute desire to know the truth, and a resolute will to carry that truth into life. Thus shall the different schools contribute, each in its own way, to the manifold wisdom of God.

I conclude by saying again that the minister should above all be a man of faith. The great need in the ministry is the need of theology, the knowledge of God, that knowing God we may interpret His ways to men, that we may find in Him the center of unity for this disordered human life, and that so we may set forward the coming of His kingdom upon earth.

PART VII

THE FUNCTIONS OF THE EPISCOPATE IN A DEMOCRACY

THE FUNCTIONS OF THE EPISCOPATE IN A DEMOCRACY

By Irving Peake Johnson

IN order to discuss this question one must first consider those principles for which a bishop functions at all. There are two widely divergent theories within the Church itself, which are very difficult to reconcile, because in a sense each is the antithesis of the other.

According to the one group, the bishop is a successor to the apostles, sent out to be a witness of certain facts and certain institutions, which were committed to the Church by Christ and of which he is for the time being a trust officer. In the words of St. Paul he is to keep the faith and to fight a good fight and to finish or round out his course. The Church for him is by no means a static institution any more than a grain of wheat is static, but just as in a grain of wheat there are certain elements which wise men cannot create so in the Church there are certain seed-facts which are of God and for which man can provide no substitute; but as the grain of wheat in the Middle Ages produced four bushels to the acre and now may produce forty, so the dynamic power of the word of God can be increased by man's provision, but one has to use the grains that have come down from Abraham to be the source of such development. To this group there are certain elements which Christ introduced that are of the Holy Ghost who is the Lord and giver of life, and for these no substitute can be accepted. In the mind of this group the Church is a biological organism and includes these basic principles.

1. That the Word was made flesh and dwelt among us.
2. That except a corn of wheat fall into the ground and die it

abideth alone, and so Christ died for us and rose from the dead—as a fact and not as fiction.

That the Holy Spirit was promised and given to the Church by Christ and that out of this gift came the sacramental life of the Church, including the grace of orders bestowed by the laying on of hands.

That by virtue of this grace so conferred man receives the forgiveness of sin, the resurrection of the body, and life everlasting. In short this group believes that the Christian religion is not merely a religious emotion, nor a philosophical speculation nor a code of ethics, but rather, that it is a new life, having its origin in Christ and its end in eternal life. To them the Episcopate is an office whose primary function is to keep that which is entrusted to its care. The bishop is a trust officer who can neither speculate with, nor give away that, which does not belong to him. And this is equally true whether the public will hear or whether they refuse to hear.

Ascending to the other group, a bishop should be a religious leader whose chief function is to read the signs of the times and to catch up and utilize whatever religious, sociological, or practical ideas are available, and by turning them into the channel of Episcopal opportunity, make the Church a crucible in which things new and old shall be so deftly mingled that there shall flow from his ministry a panacea for the ills of suffering humanity which will make the Church of Christ an effective agent in solving the perplexing problems of popular need. A bishop must be in touch with all the various sociological and ethical movements or else be relegated to those ecclesiastical catacombs where live the unburied dead.

The one is the theory of apostolic succession; the other of Episcopal success. To the one the Church is an organic body to which man must adapt himself or else suffer the consequences, just as he must adapt himself to the law of birth, of nourishment, and of environment, or else pay the penalty of his refusal. To the other the Church must adapt itself to popular demand, or itself pay the penalty of its temerity. To the one the Church is of God and cannot perish because it has the life of Christ energizing its failing strength. To the other, man is the child of God and the Church, like the Sabbath, made for him and therefore subject to such changes as his foresight may determine. There are times and places where the two views are bound to conflict, and either the Church or the demos must surrender its prerogatives.

In discussing the functions of the Episcopate in a democracy I speak as one who belongs to the first group, and who is content that the Church be true to herself and every man a liar if need be. I believe that in matters pertaining to eternal life man has such a tendency to change the truth of God into a lie and worship his own opinion rather than the Creator, that religious opinion has been usually wrong, and that the little group at the foot of the Cross is more valuable than the 5,000 who followed Christ into the desert though at great personal sacrifice, to satisfy their religious curiosity. Believing this, I advance my views upon this question, without reference to the popular demand of a world so materialistic in its desires that its spiritual insight is necessarily stupid. Not that my own views are superior but that I prefer the Message of Penti-cost to the Babel of Modern Ecclesiastical towers, and prefer to enlighten my own stupidity from that Pentecostal power house rather than walk in the sparks which flow from the occasional scintillations of prophetic genius.

The Office

The Episcopate in a democracy is not essentially different in its functions from that in an aristocracy. It is still the Church; and deacon, priest, and bishop have essentially the same functions, although such functions may be modified by the circumstances which surround them.

When the Lord founded the Church, He created a fold in which His sheep should be protected from the wolves that seek to devour them. The use of the word "sheep" is not highly complimentary. Wolves are far more intelligent and when domesticated become the most interesting of all animals; but even when the wolf becomes a dog it is still "without" in the language of Holy Scripture. The dog may be helpful to the shepherd in herding the sheep, but still it is not a part of the flock. More shepherds go to the insane asylum than any other class. Nearly all shepherds are eccentric. So the laity think that ministers are queer. It is the sheep who make them so. Sheep are foolish and exasperating and their vocabulary is limited to the highly critical but not illuminating "baa." One who enters the ministry from motives of affectionate interest in humanity, needs, like David, to find relief in playing the harp or practicing with a sling to keep himself human. Anthony Trollope testifies that when a man becomes a bishop, he loses the power of whistling. Such is the popular conception of the dehumanizing tendency of the occupation which I represent.

The Administrative Power

The Episcopate is composed, presumably, of those shepherds, who, having given a good account of themselves in the care of the sheep, are elevated to a sort of Head Shepherdship. That is having tended sheep successfully for twenty years or more, one is now promoted to be a shepherd of shepherds, a far more difficult task, as a collection of sheep is much more easily handled than an aggregation of shepherds. The task was so difficult that of our first bishops in a democracy, Bishop Provoost preferred his botanical gardens, Bishop Madison, his university students, and Bishop White, his parochial flock. I believe that Bishop Hobart was the first bishop who really made much headway in his job in this democracy. America did not take kindly to bishops at that time, and by virtue of that mechanism, known as canon law, so fettered them that their functions were extremely limited. Priests swore to obey their godly counsels, but never found that counsel particularly godly unless they themselves approved thereof. Time has somewhat altered these limitations, but it is still true that so far as actual authority goes, a bishop is more or less of a figurehead, set up between two imposing ceremonies, his consecration and his funeral, and if he attempts more, he is apt to find that he is a sign that is spoken against. As he becomes more familiar with his office, he learns that, so far as self supporting parishes are concerned, they are like self supporting sons, more or less of a law unto themselves. Bishops have not always known these limitations upon their powers at the time of their consecration, but all with whom I have been acquainted learned it before they died, and with some, the learning of this lesson had much to do with their taking off. So far as his administrative power is concerned a bishop is in much the same position as the present English sovereign. He is merely a symbol of the power which really resides in the Church, and which like the English sovereign he may have actually exercised in bygone days, but which power he wields no longer. In a democracy the bishop represents an authority which he no longer exercises. It is not necessary to his office that he should have such power, and perhaps the fact that he has been deprived of it, gives him more time and energy to devote to his other functions, but it should be distinctly recognized; otherwise the Episcopate has all the odium of a tyrant but none of the blessings. A good many people feel that royalty is expensive; I am inclined to think the money well spent, for the alternative seems to be the rather vulgar display of bourgeois or bolshevik imitations. It costs as much and is far less gracious. The Episcopate in this Church (counting salaries, expense and interest on palaces, offices, etc.,) costs us about ¾ of a million dollars a year. It is expensive, but, the question is, would the money be better spent otherwise? Whatever are the functions of the Episcopate, Bishops are not trusted with the administration of affairs. In the larger things they are fenced about with boards and kept in duress by canons. Neither boards nor canons are capable of initiative, and bishops are forcibly restrained. They get the credit of inaction, which is really due to the fact that the machine will not go. The only official who can really lead in a democracy is one who has genius for leading. This genius should be sought for among the bishops and when found should be utilized more than it is. We not only need to form an alliance of Christian bodies with which to fight the world, the flesh, and the devil—but we need a General Foch to lead the alliance. As Dr. Atwater suggests we need a Board of Strategy to direct the campaign and a leader to focus it. We are a Church with a splendid message but we lack any method of expression. We can put forth no authorized propaganda. We can set in motion no corporate action. Our General Convention is as helpless as Congress. And there is no one to speak for it *ad interim*. We have a message, a force, and a gospel—but we need personal leadership to give it expression. We are dumb and open not our mouth because each man is fearful of the other man's propaganda. We are afraid to trust any leader because he may not be of our own school of thought. We distrust archbishops because we are fearful that they will represent mere pomp and no force. If those who believe in personal leadership as the mark of efficiency would look for leadership in the Church and would seek and force those who are qualified for leadership to take the lead, we might arrive somewhere. I believe that we need to give to some bishops and some clergy and some laymen who are fit for such things the right to speak for the Church. Methodists, Roman Catholics, Christian Scientists have a definite purpose, a definite board of publication, a distinct appeal. We have none of these things, and their aggressiveness wins in an age when advertising pays. We can do none of these things, for there is no one to speak for us. We have a Presiding Bishop—no Church could have a finer one—but he is profoundly conscious of the limitations which hedge his office and too humble to overstep the limitations. Bishop Lawrence put over the pension fund because he had the ability, was given a free hand, and took it. It is a unique and solitary instance of what might be done if we had the courage, the organization, and the method. We are an aggregation of Dioceses and Parishes. Bishops and rectors function separately and are hampered in their functions by the dead hand of traditions and canonical restrictions. We trust no one to speak authoritatively for us and consequently no one does, and the triennial consulation of physicians has no more courage, no more vision, no more expression than the minimum of its composition. We have a message—but we could not use a Saul of Tarsus if we had one. We do not want an infallible Pope but we do want a fallible leader who will speak as the Holy Spirit gives him utterance. Let us have a commander in chief selected for his qualities and backed up by his constituency.

The Witnessing Function

The last words of our Lord were that the Apostles were to be witnesses of Him unto the uttermost parts of the earth. This final commission seems to carry with it two functions which are essential to the office of a bishop. He is to be a witness to those facts which are fundamental to the life of the Church, and he is to carry that witnessing function outside of the walls of Jerusalem, even to the uttermost parts of the earth. He is to keep the faith, he is to do so in an aggressive manner, for he is to fight a good fight. In the words of St. Paul, he is to hold fast the form of sound words; he is to conserve those things which he has received. It is this conserving function of the Episcopate that is very irritating to the progressive elements in the Church. The Bishop of Michigan recently put forth some very harsh strictures upon the House of Bishops because they did not agree with his views in their treatment of the Rev. Newman Smyth's rather novel proposals. I always sympathize with a banker. He has to be conservative and his conservatism is a comfort to you only when he is handling your own investments. It is comparatively easy to waste the faith in riotous thinking. It has proven a long and weary way back to the Father's house after dieting on husks. It is not pleasant to be a banker. As a rule bankers do not look as though they had an enjoyable job, nevertheless their conservatism is necessary, if industrial conditions are to be maintained, and the fruits of previous generations be enjoyed by the present. The bolsheviki do not think so. They prefer to shoot the bankers, spend the results of their conservation, and then I fancy go hungry. It would be a fine sport to shoot bankers. I have known moments when I myself would have enjoyed it, but I fancy that I would live to regret it. There are those who, having profited by the ages of conservatism during which the Church has amassed a wealth of spiritual devotion and dynamic power, are anxious now to exploit the treasures thus acquired in trying out some theory to which their speculative judgment commits them. One wonders why if the Church has been unwise in her conservatism she has anything to give to those theories which were based upon a repudiation of that which gives her strength. If it be true that these various systems which were introduced as panaceas, to remedy the evils of the Episcopal system and to save the world from bishops, have failed to demonstrate their saving power; I question whether they will be strengthened by diluted injection of Episcopal serum. I doubt the power of the injection. The college of bishops is, by the very nature of its incorporation, more or less a trust company into whose keeping was given the deposit of faith, the form of sound words, the bestowal of orders, the discipline of the faith. Some of us have been poor bankers; some of us do not like the odium of being conservative administrators of a trust fund, but I notice that even those who protest most fervently have not hesitated to take the oath which commits them to this service, nor do they carry their wrath to the point of handing back the credentials without which they could not have been inducted into office. It is, thank God, it has been the office of the Episcopate to resist all the wild and kaleidoscopic vagaries that the Church has been asked to accept as substitutes for her faith and ardour during the past 300 years. It is the business of the bishops to keep that which has been handed down to them. They are not selected as inventive geniuses, but as reliable trust officers. But a banker is not merely conservative. He is to hold his funds for the development of business. He does not put his funds into his strong box and keep them there. He invests them wisely and judiciously and so the wheels of trade go round. We need to put it out at interest, not in a wildly speculative fashion, but in a statesmanlike manner, so that the faith will be the power behind the spiritual business of the world. We are so to conserve the truth that it shall be available for use wherever it can be wisely and profitably used.   We lack a committee of investments to pass upon the wisdom of this or that measure.

The Missionary Duty

A Bishop is not a functionary but a warrior, committed to carry the war into all the world.   He must be a missionary or be false to his commission.   He has no commission to preach theories of civil or social government, however seductive and however important.   Both Christ and St. Paul seemed utterly oblivious to the social fabric of the Roman Empire, and while I am willing to concede that they were not indifferent to those conditions I believe that they relied more upon the leaven of those who accepted Christ and Him Crucified than they trusted in any direct meddling with the affairs of state.   It was this belief that made St. Paul willing to become a fool for Christ's sake.   I, however, agree with St. Paul that bishops and rectors who have given themselves to the word of God and to prayer and to preaching Christ and Him Crucified, have done more to make the world safe for democracy and democracy safe for the world, than those who have devoted themselves to the social and political problems of their day, just as I believe Francis Assisi was a more potent force in humanity than Savonarola.   If we could have a multitude who believed in Christ and Him Crucified, we would have a social state like that dreamed of in Florence but never realized, in which God's rule would be man's effort.   For if the bishops do not preach Christ and Him Crucified, who else will think it worth while?   In this field he is not restrained by boards or canons, only by the trivialities of serving tables which consume his time to no purpose.

The Power of Discipline

I am inclined to think that this unpleasant but necessary function belongs to the Episcopate and is inherent in the office. A parish priest is too intimately related to his parishioners, and too much the victim of personal relationship to administer discipline. Our canons dodge the issue and confine themselves to the discipline of the clergy when what is sorely needed is such a discipline of the laity as will rid the Church of that great army of ecclesiastical tramps, who infest our cities; belong to no regiment; assume no responsibilities; and claim all the privileges of regular soldiers, including a soldier's funeral. I would bury a Frenchman, an Englishman, or even a German soldier with military honours, but I would not give military honours to an American slacker. At least I have so interpreted my office and have defined a communicant in good standing as one who belongs to a regiment in which he performs at least a minimum of duty.

It is a sad but symbolic fact that the Episcopate should be clothed in purple and fine linen and should fare sumptuously every day. Certainly our damnation is assured if it adds to this no thought for the Lazarus who lies at our gate full of sores and being licked by the dogs of society. Bishops are like other people,—they are apt to be what people expect them to be, and I am afraid too many of us are. Dressed up in the livery of Elizabethan England, slaves to the atrocious traditions of a thoroughly secularized and opportunist Episcopate coming down through the Georgian and Victorian Eras of bad taste, bad theology, and bad manners, elected to be a sort of puppet ruler with many Mayors of the palace, committed by traditions to theories of powers that are purely fictitious, who will deliver us from the emptiness of this bondage! What suggestions would I make to remedy these conditions?

1st.—To get rid of the bad traditions of the Roman and Anglican Episcopate and return to Apostolic simplicity. There are three words derived from the same root,—Simplicity, duplicity, complexity;—one fold, two folds, many folds. When you make a perfectly plain man of God into a lord imperial or spiritual you put upon him a burden that even the most stable can scarcely bear, for man being in honour hath no understanding but is compared to the beasts that perish. As Canon McCord says in his autobiography, "No progress has ever been made in the English Church by the aid of the Episcopate but in spite of it." The Bishop is to be a conservative in the faith but he ought to be a radical in human interest.

2nd.—I am inclined to favor such a revision in the ordinal as will place the witnessing missionary and disciplinary functions where they belong and adapt the administrative functions to a world in which imperialism has given way to the constitutional. There was nothing, in my opinion, particularly sacrosanct in the atmosphere of Edward VI and his greedy uncles nor in that of Elizabeth and her penurious policies. Why not face the question that bishops do not govern in this Church, and recognize that we place upon them a fictitious power which consumes their time in attempting to do that which the canons effectively prevent them from doing. What we need is a clearer and more definite statement of what a bishop is to do, not what it is pretended that he is to do. Let the Church be frank and if it prefers to entrust the administration of affairs to boards and committees. (I do not admire them. They are as a rule indolent, timid, and inefficient; but the temporal administration of the Church is not of primary importance.) Let us leave the service of tables, let us put the secular administration of the Diocese into other hands. It is something that our laity can and ought to do, for the laity surely ought to do something and what better than the task of administering hospitals, schools, invested funds, drives for building and extension, relieve the bishops of their purely fictitious power in these temporal things and put it on the shoulders where it belongs and let us carry out the purely spiritual functions of the Word and of prayer. (At present a bishop is compelled to cut short his petitions to the Almighty and to transfer this service of intercession to his wealthy laymen.) But above all things let us trust one another in the household of faith and put into the hands of somebody the power to carry on our campaign against the world, the flesh, and the devil and to set before the American people this fact, that we have all the faith that is held by them in fragmentary fashion, and that we have a household in which the emphasis is not upon intellectual agreement (as it was at the Reformation) but is put upon reverence for God and fraternity with those who are of the household of faith.

3rd.—I would put an age limit beyond which bishops could not serve.

It is true that some bishops are effective after they are 68, but I believe the best interests of the Church would be served if bishops and rectors were forced to retire at that age. As a Church we are so considerate of everybody's feelings but the Lord's, that I will guarantee to get any candidate for Holy Orders (that has not had a state prison sentence or is not a mental defective) into the ministry in some diocese; or, if he be elevated to high office, to keep him there, until death do them part. An aggressive army needs personal leadership from among its regularly commissioned officers, a definite board of strategy to execute authority, a clearly defined commission for all those who serve, and a fixed time limit for those in authority.

We need an effective organization in which somebody is trusted to go ahead and in which those who criticise and those who slack and those who are in revolt shall come forth and show us a better way, or for ever after hold their peace.

THE FUNCTIONS OF THE EPISCOPATE IN A DEMOCRACY

By John Howard Melish

WHEN Archbishop Ceretti, Under Secretary of State at the Vatican and the highest prelate of the Roman Catholic Church to visit America, landed in New York, he gave an interesting interview to the reporters, in which among other things he referred to the recent visit paid to the Pope by President Wilson. "It was an historic day," he said, "when the head of the great American republic met the head of that old democratic institution founded by Christ nineteen centuries ago. America is looked upon today as the hope of the world." That old democratic institution founded by Christ! Is it not significant that the Archbishop sought to commend his Church to the American people on the ground of its democratic lineage? It is not without significance that he also finds the hope of the world, not in his Church but in this American democracy. Even representatives of the most reactionary and conservative institution on earth, the Church of Rome, are beginning to recognize that the pole-star of the twentieth century is democracy.

The Function of the Episcopate in a democracy is my subject. There are three functions of the Episcopate in a democracy. First it is to become itself democratic; its second function is to democratize the Church; and its third function is to democratize the democracy.

I

The Episcopate is itself to be democratized. The Archbishop rightly called the Church founded by Christ nineteen centuries ago a democracy. Imperialism ruled the Rome, and aristocracy the Israel of His day. His society was to resemble neither. Jesus called the Twelve unto Him and said, " Ye know that the rulers of the Gentiles lord it over them, and their great ones exercise authority over them. Not so shall it be among you: but whosoever would become great among you shall be minister; and whosoever would be first among you shall be your servant." "Call no man your father on the earth: for one is your father." "I call you not servants: ye are my friends." In spite of these injunctions do men with episcopal ambitions among us desire the position in order to "exercise authority", or in order to become the bond servants of the democracy? And do we turn in the comfirmation office and say, as though the words of Jesus had never been spoken, "Right Reverend Father in God, I present unto thee these persons?" *

Can the Episcopate become democratic? There is a consensus of opinion to-day among intelligent men as to the origin of the institution. None but the ecclesiastical caveman believes any longer in apostolic succession. All scholarly High Churchmen, so I am informed by one of them, recognize now that the episcopate came into existence, not by superimposition from above but by development of the Catholic Church from within. The democratic society of Jesus developed in the course of centuries into the imperialistic institution of Innocent III. One stage of that long process was the diocesan episcopate. The only suggestion of democracy retained by the institution was the manner of election to it; the bishop was elected by the populace in mass meeting. The Papacy finally stripped it even of this democratic feature, and the Kings of England saw to it that it remained undemocratic, after the national revolt against the tyranny of the Popes. Can an institution which came out of an undemocratic and imperialistic age and has for centuries been the ally of divine-right kings become democratic? Continental Protes-

---

* S. Matt.   20:26-7.   Idem. 23:9.   S. John 15:14.

tantism answered with an almost universal negative. With characteristic British compromise England retained the episcopate at the Reformation but subordinated it to the State. She also freed the clergy from the overlordship of the bishop by changing the mediaeval ordination vow of unqualified obedience to one of submission to his godly admonition and godly judgment; which leaves the clergy, not the bishop, the necessity of deciding as to whether the admonition and judgment are godly or ungodly.

When we organized ourselves as an independent Church in this country in 1789 this question of the democratic character of the episcopate was, next to the question of the unity of the churches in the thirteen states, the supreme question. It was the decision of the convention that the institution of the episcopate could be adapted to a democracy, provided it was stripped of authority, elected by the people, and put under law. Some one has wittily remarked of the Church of England that it has four notes: Bishops without authority, religion without Mystery, an open Bible, and a closed hell. Like many generalizations it is more humourous than true. But it is true of the American Episcopal Church that it deliberately stripped its bishops of authority. If he is a man of personal leadership, great wisdom, a preacher of ability, and a councillor gifted with insight and sympathy, his individual authority is great. "The leaders lead." Of sixty-one canons of the General Church twelve relate to the office and trial of bishops. Our democratic forefathers had a healthy suspicion of the English episcopate and in bringing it to the land of freedom they put it clearly and definitely beneath law, just as they did their colonial governors. John Wesley, an obey-your-bishop Churchman, modeled his Superintendent after the Anglican bishop. The Methodist Church, after much experience, has now stripped its bishops of authority, has given to the presiding elder the episcopal power of appointment, and is now engaged in bringing this demi-espiscopos under democratic control. Even the Roman Catholic Church has now put forth a decree which went into effect last Whitsunday, aimed to free the parish priest somewhat from episcopal arbitrariness. The reign of persons is tyranny, the reign of law is liberty.

In the Episcopal Church as in the democratic state all government derives its power from the consent of the governed. The High Churchman affirms the contrary and finds the seat of authority in a class. They are aristocrats, not democrats, in their ecclesiology. But the history of the Church in this country, whatever may be the judgment of St. Cyprian, or Bishop Seabury, gives little support for this dogma. The men who drafted the constitution and canons of the Protestant Episcopal Church in the United States of America were in many cases the same men who later drafted the Constitution of the United States. They believed in local self-government, in state sovereignty, in a government of delegated powers. There were some in the constitutional convention of 1789 who wanted a stronger central government, and there were others who wanted a weaker central government than we possess. What we have is a compromise between Hamiltonians and Jeffersonians. So in the Church our organic law is a compromise between Bishop White and Bishop Seabury. White wanted no House of Bishops at all and declared that it would prove itself a menace in the future. Seabury refused to join with the other states at all unless he could sit in a house removed from laymen and lower clergy. A House of Bishops elected for life and subject to no recall, sitting independently of the other Orders, co-ordinate in theory, but practically wielding a veto on its equal, was a compromise. It has worked so unsatisfactorily that when the Church formed the Provincial Synods it struck the House of Bishops our of its proposed legislation without a single objection, and provided one democratic assembly. The Methodist Church allows its Bishops to have their own assembly for certain purposes, but gives it no power to overrule the will of the church indefinitely. The day is coming when we must abolish or define our House of Lords.

Eternal vigilance is the price of the liberty wherewith Christ has made us free. There are some dioceses in which the clergy demand the right to nominate the bishop and accord to the laity only the right of ratifying their choice. This is a violation of the fundamental right of democracy, which makes the election of a bishop the right of the people, not of a clerical caste.

What would happen if the Governor of the State attempted to nominate a mayor or a dog-catcher in one of the smallest towns, and graciously announced that its people might select one of his partisans? Republicans and Democrats alike would unite to tell his Excellency to mind his own business. There are some dioceses in which the bishop claims the right to submit to vacant parishes the names of men from whom they may choose a rector. Must not a High bishop, forsooth, have a High Church diocese, or a Low Church bishop have a Low Church diocese! Well, he may get it, but the Church loses a democratic diocese.

There are some dioceses in which no legislation, no reports to convention can be offered unless the bishop has first given his approval. Imagine any Mayor, Governor, or President of the United States claiming for his office such an undemocratic method of procedure.

Did Richmond approve of Christian men speaking on special occasions, or not? Every one thought it did at the time, and some twenty odd 'Catholics' fled to Rome as a result of letting down the bars. Since then some bishops had a happy thought: Richmond put up the bars, and placed in their episcopal hands a power they never possessed before! The political boss, John Y. McKane, said, "Supreme Court injunctions don't go in my district." And we sent him to Sing Sing. Some bishops say, "Canon XX doesn't go in my jurisdiction." And we tamely submit. In the State, were an official to set aside the law because he did not personally approve of it, we would secure a mandamus. In the Church there is no court to mandamus a bishop. The only thing left the man for whom it is a matter of conscience is to proceed without the episcopal consent, and be treated as one that "stirreth up the people and refuseth to pay tribute unto Caesar."

What shall we say of the bishop in the missionary jurisdiction? Once upon a time the missionary was in danger of being eaten by the heathen; his fear now is lest he be devoured by his bishop. The Church affords no protection of law to its devoted missionaries. The House of Bishops defeated the effort of the Deputies to curb the missionary bishops even by requiring them to consult the Committee of Advice in certain matters. Only the general high character of our missionary bishops has protected the clergy from grievous hurt and the Church from serious injury. Every ship must have a Captain. But the captain is accountable on reaching port for his treatment of the crew at sea. The captains of our missionary ships have all responsibility and no accountability.

In this day of "open covenants openly arrived at" will not the democratic bishops take up again the fight to open the doors of the House of Bishops? No democracy in the world retains a senate sitting like a Curia or Star Chamber. If their deliberations concern the spiritual democracy the democracy should hear them: if they do not concern the democracy let there be "silence in heaven about the space of half an hour."

II

The second function of the episcopate in a democracy is to make the Church democratic.

In the analysis the Church is the people. Roman Catholicism believes in two churches; the officials who govern and teach, the ecclesia docens; the people who are governed and taught. Our church rejecting this as unchristian holds the Church to be the beloved community "the blessed company of all faithful people." Bishops, priests, and deacons—yes, even deaconesses, are the executives of the spiritual community, its public servants as we say in democracies. The people get the kind of public servants they deserve. So the people get the kind of bishops they deserve.

There are dioceses in which no man without independent means can become bishop. The people expect him to live in a palace and yet pay him the salary of a floor-walker. What is the result? Only rich men need apply! Or should a poor man be eligible a group of rich laymen underwrite the income he needs over and above the salary the diocese pays. When the bishop spends most of his time outside his diocese, when his words on any social question sound like utterances of a subsidized newspaper, the people have themselves to blame. Let every diocese pay its bishop a living wage.

The Bishop of London once told me that he determined when appointed bishop to live simply among the poor, rather than at Fulham, but that he was dissuaded from carrying out his plan by the poor curates of his diocese. They wanted their bishop to live in a palace.

Let the men who are to become the bishops of the Church in this new democratic age refuse to be subsidized, however good the intentions of the rich laymen: let them live within their salaries as bishops: let them not be classed with the rich but with the plain people of America. Then will they help mightily to make the people of the Church, rich and poor alike, democratic. Why should Victor Hugo's Christ-like picture of the Bishop of S— be a work of fiction and not a fact? One day he arrived at Senez mounted on a donkey. The Mayor of the city met him and watched him dismount with scandalized eyes. A few townspeople were laughing around him. "Mr Mayor and gentlemen," said the bishop, "I see what it is that shocks you. You consider it great pride for a poor priest to ride an animal which our Saviour once rode. I did so from necessity, I assure you and not from vanity."

III

The third function of the episcopate in a democracy is to make the democracy democratic.

A distinguished member of the English episcopate complained on a visit to this country before the war that a wretched little Welsh attorney by the name of Lloyd George, had compelled him to determine the land values of his see which had not been valued since the 12th century. When the Archbishop of York was here recently, he said the upper classes of England knew that there could not be a return of the pre-war conditions, and they were prepared to give way to the more democratic conditions that would come with peace. The new democracy is coming all over the world. The bishops can oppose it, as in the case of the Bishop of S—, or interpret it as Dr. Lang is doing. Or they can become apostles of land reform like our own fine democrat, Charles D. Williams; or socialists like the late Frank Spalding. All democratic bishops, each in his own way, help the democracy to become more democratic.

Two episcopal utterances are before the World at the present moment. One is the so-called Archbishop's Report on Christianity and Industrial Problems and the other is the recent statement of the four Roman Catholic bishops on Social Reconstruction. These last desire a society in which there shall be a "more just distribution of wealth in the interest of the labourer." For the fulfilment of this aim they recommend a variety of social reforms. They even go so far as to look forward to the abolition of the wage system to a great extent, and the ownership by the workers themselves of the instruments of production. This episcopal statement has been received with joy by the working people within the Roman Catholic Church, who since Leo XIII's historic utterance on the relations between capital and labour, have felt that their hierarchy had put its light under a bushel.

The Archbishop's Report on Christianity and Industrial problems is concerned with what its Chairman, the Bishop of Winchester, calls "the coming democracy." "Much in the Report," they say, "will come to many churchmen as an unwelcome challenge and demand." Their aim, is to "do something to take out of the way of large numbers of God's people stumblingblocks which have made faith in God and the reception of Christ more difficult to them." In the interest of religion and the new democracy the Archbishop, like a "trumpet call," summons the Church, to take heed to the manifold ways in which it is frequently violating, in this industrial epoch the principles of human value and human comradeship. We are conscious, they say, of "the lamentable failure in the Church's recent witness." "We have been content with the ambulance work when we ought to have been assaulting the strongholds of evil. We have allowed avarice and selfishness and grinding competition to work havoc over the broad spaces of human life. We want a strenuous reaffirmation of the principles of justice, mercy, and brotherhood as sovereign over every department of human life."

Here are two notable efforts on the part of the episcopate, Roman and Anglican, to function in the interest of democratising the democracy. Does some one think: The writer is is inconsistent? He repudiates the dictation of the episcopate in his first section: he acclaims it in matters of social interest. Not so. In putting forth their report the Archbishop of Canterbury says that they appointed their "best and strongest to deal with these industrial matters." Of twenty-eight members on the committee there were four bishops, five other clergymen, seventeen laymen, and two women. Though the Roman Catholic bishops alone sign their programme of Social Reconstruction it is generally known that it is the work of many, especially of Professor Ryan, the most eminent Roman Catholic economist and sociologist in America. In other words the episcopate claims no superior knowledge or authority. As Christ enjoined His apostles to do, these bishops have sat at the feet of social service and learned. They have democratized themselves, and therefore are in a position to democratize the democracy.

The next episcopal move on the great chess board of modern democratic life belongs to our House of Bishops. The Anglicans have spoken, the Romanists have spoken, what will the American bishops say as to social reconstruction and industrial democracy? An utterance on any other subject will receive little attention; an utterance on this subject is awaited with

eager anticipation. I am not in the confidence of those gentlemen, but I venture to say this. If the next Pastoral Letter
is written by one bishop, with the criticism of two others, in
the closing hours of a General Convention, it will go the way
of all other pastorals in these last years; read, as the canons
require, but "unwept, unhonored, and unsung." The day for
ex cathedra statements has gone by. The day for democratic
utterances has come. Let our bishops sit at the feet of science,
as Labour in England says it did, as the Archbishop's committee and the Roman Catholic bishops have done: let them
listen to the voice of God speaking today in the common people
of the world; and then let them speak to the Church and their
generation. The world wants no pastoral letters that issue
from "great ones exercising authority." But common people
everywhere are hungry and thirsty for living words of council
and understanding from those who are among us as One that
served.

The war has liberated mighty forces which, to use one
of Mr. Wilson's illuminating phrases, "do not threaten, they
operate." They have operated in Russia in 1917 as they
operated in France in 1789, as they will operate in America,
if we take no heed to our ways. The Church that becomes
identified with the things of this world, money, property,
privilege, is destined to fall the moment the axe of democracy
is laid at its root. The Church that serves, even though it
die, will live in the new democracy. We are not going back
to pre-war conditions either in Church or State; we are going
forward to more Christlike deeds and a more Christlike spirit.
The old leaves are falling, sometimes shaken by the winds
without, sometimes pushed off by the rising sap within. I
have confidence that the Church of God will be the same tree
that has stood through the centuries, but it will be of larger
girth, and wider reach of limb and richer fruitage; and that
the leaves of this tree will be for the healing of the Nations.

THE FUNCTIONS OF THE EPISCOPATE IN A DEMOCRACY

By Bernard Iddings Bell

THE more I have thought over this very interesting topic which has been assigned to me for discussion the more it has become evident to me that before it can be discussed with any lucidity another subject must first be considered; namely, the true relationship between revealed religion and democracy. To that subject therefore let us address ourselves, trusting that out of it may come a clearer perception of the relationship of the *Episcopate* to democracy.

First of all, let us very clearly see that democracy has no effect whatever upon Almighty God. There seems to be present in the minds of many good people a notion that the universe revolves around the human race. It does nothing of the sort. God is the center of all things. His laws are immutable, and His sovereignty absolute. He will reign regardless of any human plebescites; and His will is not subject to human referendum and recall. The fact that upon this bit of star-dust, revolving around a quite insignificant sun, certain groups of people abolish monarchies, dethrone nobilities, bowl over plutocracies, and proclaim that all the people shall rule politically and industrially will cause, I take it, no great upheaval in the courts of the heavens.

There is nothing sacred about democracy. The voice of the people is merely the voice of the people. It is by no means the voice of God. It seems certain that all that God is interested in about democracy is to see whether democracy will obey His laws any better than plutocracy did, or than feudalism did, or than autocracy did. In fact God is very little interested in what may be the form of government on this earth. He is concerned only with whether men and women obey His eternal and unchangeable laws designed for their welfare, happiness, and spiritual growth.

The eternal law of God for men is that they shall grow great by sacrificial love and small by selfish acquisitiveness. The commandment that men love one another is the lesson taught by secular as well as religious history, by reason, and by revelation culminating in Jesus Christ. When kings ruled as the vice-gerents of God, loving their people and beloved by them, their kingdoms prospered. When kings began to think that they ruled by divine right, and force supplanted love, they perished. God wiped them out. When feudalism was, as it once was, an organization of society whereby men mutually bore burdens for one another, when peasants supported lords who supported peasants, it produced the most glorious thirteenth century. When selfish seeking supplanted mutual-loving responsibility, it perished. God destroyed it. It is conceivable that even a capitalist state might be pleasing to God, if in very truth the capitalists regarded their holdings as really and truly trusts from God for the benefit of their fellows. The fact that they did not this, but began to think that they had inherent rights to their private property, has necessitated the present world maelstrom, wherein God is destroying plutocracy. Now comes democracy on the scene. If democracy is inspired of mutual love between all men it will live. If, however, it is inspired by selfish materialistic grubbing for pelf, as it seems to me it mostly is at this moment, God is going to smash it too.

The only thing which ever has produced, or ever can produce, loving and sacrificing people is not a form of government at all, but the Christian religion. It is very hard for human beings to be sacrificing. For one to deny one's self, curb one's selfish animal body, and shout defiance at the canny wisdom of the world, is a tremendous job. While some individuals have been able to do it without Christianity, in all ages, it still remains true that the great masses of the simple, ordinary people have never been able to do it except when they were gripped tight by that same Christian religion. It is therefore the one great service possible for the Church to render democracy that it motivate democracy with ideas of service from Christ, and so save it from ruining itself. That this may be, the Christian religion must be zealously protected by its guardians from degeneracy, liberalistic camouflage, and the modern tendency to pretty prattle.

This Christian religion which has been so powerful in the past in impelling men and women to sacrificing lives and which must be preserved for the new age is a *personal comradeship* with God through Jesus Christ. Its simplicity and integrity have throughout the ages been safeguarded by the following dogmas:

1. The doctrine of the Holy Trinity, with which is intimately bound up the doctrine of the Incarnation. Briefly, it maintains that the great creator God, the maker of immutable law, who is incomprehensible to the limited mind of man, and the great Comrade, Jesus Christ, Deity revealed in comprehensible terms of human leadership, and the spirit which dwells in human breasts and speaks to them, which is called the Holy Spirit, are all of them God, and the same God. This is especially valuable to simple folk such as those who rule democracies in that it makes God, in Christ and in the Holy Spirit, intimate, vital, simple to every one who seeks God at all, and effectually prevents that devitalizing of God which is the weakness of all modern liberalism as it has been of medieval liberalism and ancient liberalism.

2. The Sacraments and Prayer, as the means of mystical yet exceedingly real contact of man with God. Of these, Prayer is essentially talking with God rather than asking favours of God, while the Sacraments are means whereby the Invisible Christ reaches out and touches physically the physical part of man, thus making the presence of His Spirit to man's spirit felt, much in the manner that a handshake or a kiss makes souls touch as well as bodies. The advantage of sacraments is that they make God's sanctioning touch real

and vital to the average man, the strength and hope of Democracy, who is a quite simple person capable of feeling a sacramental Christ vividly but quite incapable of meeting an abstracted and intellectualized Christ.

3. The Resurrection as a complete vindication of the wisdom of sacrifice, as perfect evidence of the final triumph of unselfishness and the final overthrow of the worldly wisdom of compromise with evil. Thus is given eternal sanction to the morality of sacrifice, a morality which finds expression in various things, all taught by Christ's own words and His example, among which may be listed: a. the indissolubility of marriage, which involves the sacrifice of parents for their children; b. the holding of all wealth in trust, thus subserving property to human personality; c. the indispensability of *caritas*, which is simply the Christian name for an impulse to sacrifice, as the solution of industrial and social ills; and d. the sovereignty of God over the state and an insistence that the state be based on sacrificing fraternity.

Into all this we have gone at some length, for if Christianity has any function in a democracy that function must be to help the simple citizens or *fraires* of the democracy to find in Christ, the Incarnate God, through prayer and sacraments, such power as will enable them, realizing their comradeship with the Resurrected One, to live, in marriage, industry, and politics, the sacrificing life.

Now possibly we can see what is the function of the Episcopate in a democracy. In the Providence of God the preservation and the supervision of this religion, needed in a democracy as it has always been needed under every former type of government, has been placed in the hands of the Episcopate. Therefore we may say that in a democracy the function of the Episcopate is to preserve and set forward the Christian religion and the Christian morality, unchanged and unchanging, that men may perceive what things they ought to do and be and may obtain from God, through Christ, grace and strength faithfully to fulfil the same.

This is a conclusion so obvious that it seems absurd to have to state it. Yet there are, doubtless, people to whom it sounds like a great novelty,—so far have we fallen even among our intelligent folk from any real comprehension of what Christianity is and what Christian bishops, the guardians of the faith, really are committed to uphold.

Let us take an example or two. Suppose a bishop finds that a certain Church, for the religion of which he is held accountable by God, invites a Unitarian to preach in the pulpit, a procedure which advertises plainly that the parish or its rector no longer considers the Deity of Christ of any importance. It would seem to be the function of the Bishop to rise up and rebuke and even to excommunicate, if it remained refractory, the offending parish; and if the parish said that democracy demanded such broad-minded or shallow-minded tolerance, the Bishop ought kindly but firmly to say that then democracy was wrong and to be rebuked. If a priest of the Church in a diocese persisted in remarrying divorced people, contrary to Christ's express command, and offered as excuse that emerging democracy demanded the destruction of the Christian home, then a bishop ought certainly to say that democracy might do that at its own peril if it wished but that the Church could not and would not allow its clergy to lend their blessing to such impious nonsense. And if a priest of the Church declared he was through with the Doctrine of the Resurrection and so with "such nonsense as the Sacrament of Holy Communion," and neglected to provide it regularly for the faithful, the Bishop ought in no uncertain manner to maintain that such a priest, Democrat or not, had no place in the Church at all and had far better for the sake of his own integrity become an ethical culture teacher. These are some examples of what negatively the function of a bishop in a democracy ought to be. In fact the Episcopal Church makes a bishop vow before God that he will do just this sort of protecting.

However, it will never do, in this heathen country and heathen age, for a bishop merely to protect the faith by banishing erroneous and false doctrines. He ought to be leading in proclaiming the true doctrine. He cannot, thank God, in a democracy force men to be even nominally Christians. The democratic state will never give a bishop police powers. His position does, however, furnish him a pedestal from which he can, if so be he is a real bishop and a real democrat, persuade men to Christ, and solemnly warn them if, personally or nationally or internationally, they are denying Christ. Democracy needs Christian prophets. It gets nowhere by a collective pulling on a common boot-strap. It needs prophets. Such preëminently bishops ought to be. They must love common folk and simple ways and believe in government by common folk and preach to common folk with loving leadership. They must not follow. He who follows in a democracy is nobody. They must lead, argue, invoke, provoke, persuade, discuss, and above all teach, in terms of the day in which they live, in terms of the hopes, the fears, the joys, the sorrows, the problems, the difficulties, of the common people about him the unchanging and constructive principles of the Faith committed to him to proclaim. And he must further surround himself with lesser prophets, clerical and lay, who will help him do this thing, that democrats may have that eternal life which consists in knowing God and Jesus Christ whom He hath sent. And he and they must preach never themselves and their wisdom but always Jesus Christ and Him Crucified, and lead men to Him, in prayer and Sacrament, that they may indeed know Him and what He would have them to do.

It is very few of our bishops today who can find opportunity for this sort of thing. They are for the most part tied down to administer properties. They must be business men and organizers. It may not be an unmixed blessing when democracy takes away properties and endowments, as it is certain to do. It may free the bishops. Possibly in the interim they might be freed if our dioceses were so organized that vicars-general might handle finance in the name of the diocese and take this burden off Episcopal shoulders. It does seem queer how some bishops hang on to their temporal privileges and duties, kissing their manacles, as it were. One sometimes wonders if some of them do not recognize that they dare not be real bishops and so thank God that they have temporalties in which to hide their incompetence from themselves. However, these are but few. Most of the bishops chafe at their chains.

The Church should help to free them, and then say to them: "Be real Bishops and Shepherds of the flock. Defend the Faith. Persuade Democracy toward Christ. Stir up the gift that is in you. Forget not to take frequent counsel with one another, since it is to the Episcop*ate* and not to the Episcop*os* that the keys were once committed. Hold fast that which is committed unto you. Then, whether Democracy heeds and lives, or fails to heed and perishes from off the earth, you will have done your part and be worthy of being numbered with those blessed bishops who in their day did, and did well, that which in your day it is committed to you to do."

In the name of the simple folk, the "little people," the ones upon whom the success of all democracies depend; in the name of those great, simple men, the soldiers and sailors of our land, with so many of whom I have become intimately acquainted, I ask for bishops who shall preserve for us the simple faith, freed from the hazy mazes of liberalistic camouflage, and who, having thus taught us the things of God, shall come down with us into the marketplace and help us fight to bring God's will to pass.

Printed in the United States of America